Louise Manning Hodgkins

A Guide to the Study of Nineteenth Century Authors

Louise Manning Hodgkins

**A Guide to the Study of Nineteenth Century Authors**

ISBN/EAN: 9783337280901

Printed in Europe, USA, Canada, Australia, Japan

Cover: Foto ©Thomas Meinert / pixelio.de

More available books at **www.hansebooks.com**

# A Guide to the Study of

# Nineteenth Century Authors.

BY

## LOUISE MANNING HODGKINS,

Professor of English Literature in Wellesley College.

————∞∘⦂⊙⦂∘∞————

BOSTON, U.S.A.,

D. C. HEATH & CO., PUBLISHERS.

1895.

# PREFACE.

⸺••⸺

THIS work was originally prepared for the students of Wellesley College in the form of leaflets to accompany a course of lectures on Authors of the Nineteenth Century. At the request of the class, accustomed to use them in a well equipped library, the blank pages were retained for the outline of the lecture and the addition of new material to the books of reference. It was not until a frequent demand for single copies from teachers, leaders of literary clubs, and students of other colleges, led the author to believe that they might have a more extended usefulness, that their publication was contemplated.

It is hoped that the book will be found suggestive to the teacher of Literature, Rhetoric, or Essay, who finds himself too hard pressed for time to make for himself a careful selection from the author he is presenting, and to the less mature student from whom a judicious choice from a voluminous writer is rarely to be expected.

The papers have been arranged in an order to remind the thoughtful student of the great contemporaneous, political, and social interests which have found expression in the revolutionary energy of the Georgian and the scientific earnestness of the Victorian era. The books of reference have been selected from many times their number, and always because the writer recommended offers a distinctly fresh thought in the criticism or analysis of the author. While every good reader is aware that the poorest thing an author has said is often better than the best the critics have said about him, he also knows that the opinion of a good critic goes far to establish in the mind of the student a worthy basis of sound judgment.

The author will gratefully receive notice of valuable books of reference which may have been overlooked, or which were altogether wanting in her studies in a library which, though generous, was not exhaustive.

L. M. H.

WELLESLEY COLLEGE, Sept. 25, 1888.

# CONTENTS.

—◦✦◦—

## ENGLISH AUTHORS.

## AMERICAN AUTHORS.

# ENGLISH AUTHORS.

# A Guide to the Study of Nineteenth Century Authors.

By LOUISE MANNING HODGKINS,

PROFESSOR OF ENGLISH LITERATURE IN WELLESLEY COLLEGE.

Copyright, 1887.

## SIR WALTER SCOTT, 1771-1832.

### Biographical Writings.

*Chief Biographer of Scott*, JOHN GIBSON LOCKHART, 1838.

*Other Contributions to Scott's Biography.*

Domestic Manners and Private Life of Sir Walter Scott. By James Hogg. 1834.

Recollections of Sir Walter Scott. Fraser's Magazine. 1835.

Sir Walter Scott. By R. H. Hutton. (English Men of Letters Series.) 1878.

Great Novelists. By James Crabb Watt. 1880.

*Scott's Home.* — Homes and Haunts of the British Poets. By William Howitt. Vol. II.

Miscellanies : Abbotsford. By Geoffrey Crayon (W. Irving).

Lands of Scott. By James F. Hunnewell.

### Significant Facts in the Life of Scott.

Border Ancestry.     Precocious Imagination.

Education in Classics and Law.

Publication of the Lay of the Last Minstrel.   1805

Publication of Waverley.   1814.

The Establishment of Abbotsford.

### A Group of Contemporary English Novelists.

Fanny Burney (Madame D'Arblay),
1752–1840.
William Godwin, 1756–1836.
Anne Radcliffe, 1764–1823.
Maria Edgeworth, 1767–1849.
Jane Austen, 1775–1817.
Jane Porter, 1776–1850.
Mrs. Trollope, 1778–1836.
Theodore Hook, 1788–1841.

### Selections from the Poetry of Sir Walter Scott.

#### BALLADS.

*From Minstrelsy of the Scottish Border, 1802–1803.*

William and Helen.    Eve of St. John.
Glenfinlas.    Cadyow Castle.

#### CHIEF ROMANTIC POEMS.

Lay of the Last Minstrel, 1805.
Marmion, 1808.
Lady of the Lake, 1810.

#### LESS FAMOUS POEMS.

Vision of Don Roderick, 1811.
Rokeby, 1813.
Bridal of Triermain, 1813.
Lord of the Isles, 1814.
Harold the Dauntless, 1817.

NOTE. — For poems from novels, see appendix to Sproat's "Scott as a Poet."

SELECTIONS FROM LADY OF THE LAKE.

*Delineative Pictures.*

| | |
|---|---|
| Malcolm Graeme, | Canto II., 25. |
| Blanche of Devon, | " IV., 21–27. |
| Ellen and Fitz James, | { " IV., 16–20. |
| | { " VI., 27–29. |
| Fitz James and Roderick Dhu, | " IV., 30–31. |
| Clan Alpine starting from Ambush, | " V., 9. |

*Descriptive Pictures*

| | |
|---|---|
| Sunset in the Trosachs, | Canto I., 11–14. |
| The Lodge, | " I., 26–27. |
| Sunrise on Loch Katrine. | " III., 2. |
| Entrance to the Castle, and Robin Hood, | " V., 21–22. |
| Fitz James and Roderick Dhu, | " V., 12–16. |
| Battle Scene in the Trosachs, | " VI., 15–22. |

*Songs.*

| | |
|---|---|
| Soldier, Rest, | Canto I., 31. |
| Hail to the Chief, | " II., 19. |
| Coronach, | " III., 16. |
| Ave Maria, | " III., 29. |

**Ten Selected Novels.**

| | |
|---|---|
| Waverley, 1814. | Heart of Midlothian. 1818. |
| Guy Mannering, 1815. | Bride of Lammermoor, 1819 |
| Antiquary, 1816. | Ivanhoe, 1819. |
| Old Mortality, 1816. | Kenilworth, 1821. |
| Rob Roy, 1817. | Talisman, 1825. |

Number of Novels written by Sir Walter Scott, 27.
Date of publication, 1814–1831.

## A Group of Scott's Friends.

James Hogg.

William Laidlaw.

Jane Austen.

King George IV.

John Wilson.

Henry Brougham.

Washington Irving.

William Wordsworth.

Robert Southey.

William Erskine.

Joanna Bailey.

George Canning.

## Selected Books of Reference on Sir Walter Scott.

Jeffrey's Critical Essays. From Edinburgh Review. 1805–1813.

On the Dramatic Powers of the Author of Waverley. Blackwood's Magazine. February, 1826.

Noctes Ambrosianæ. By John Wilson. 1833.

Sir Walter Scott. By Allan Cunningham. North American Review. April, 1833.

Miscellanies. (The Genius of Sir Walter Scott.) By Harriet Martineau. 1836.

Miscellanies. (Scott.) By Thomas Carlyle. 1837–1838.

Walter Scott : Has History gained by his Writings? Fraser's Magazine. September, 1847.

Lectures on Poetical Literature. By D. M. Moir. 1856.

British Poets. Vol. II., Lect. VII. (Criticism of Scott's Poetry.) By H. W. Reed. 1857.

Scott's Heroines : Diana Vernon. Macmillan's Magazine. May–October, 1870.

A Century of Great Poets from 1750. Blackwood's Magazine. August, 1871.

Scott's Birthday. The Nation. August 17, 1871.

Lands of Scott. (For outlines and local allusions of Scott's poems and novels.) By James F. Hunnewell. 1871.

On Scott's Words.   (From Cornhill Magazine.)   Littell's
Living Age.   October, 1871.
The Scott Centenary at Edinburgh.   By M. D. Conway.
Harper's.   February, 1872.
Hours in a Library.   (Some Words about Sir Walter Scott.)
By Leslie Stephen.   1875.
Lectures on Poetry.   By Sir F. H. Doyle.   1877.
Sir Walter Scott, and the Romantic Reaction.   By Julia
Wedgwood.   Contemporary Review.   October, 1878.
Fiction Fair and Foul.   By John Ruskin.   Nineteenth Cen-
tury.   June, 1880.
Aspects of Poetry.   (The Homeric Spirit of Walter Scott.)
By J. S. C. Shairp.   1881.
The Waverley Dictionary.   By May Rogers.   1886.
Letters to Dead Authors.   (Scott.)   By Andrew Lang.   1886

# A Guide to the Study of Nineteenth Century Authors.

### By LOUISE MANNING HODGKINS,

PROFESSOR OF ENGLISH LITERATURE IN WELLESLEY COLLEGE.

Copyright, 1887.

## CHARLES LAMB, 1775-1834.

### Biographies of Lamb.

Memorial of Charles Lamb. By Thomas Noon Talfourd, 1848.

Charles Lamb: a Memoir. By Bryan Waller Procter. 1866.

The Life. Letters, and Writings of Charles Lamb. Edited by Percy Fitzgerald. 1876.

Charles Lamb. By Alfred Ainger. (English Men of Letters Series.) 1882.

### Significant Facts in the Life of Lamb.

Education in Christ's Hospital. 1782–1789.

Clerkship in the India House. 1792–1825.

Guardianship of Mary Lamb.

Publication of the Essays of Elia. 1823.

Literary friendship with Wordsworth and Coleridge.

Retired Life in London and its Suburbs.

## A Group of Charles Lamb's Friends.

S. T. Coleridge.

James White.

Samuel Le Grice.

Robert Manning.

William Wordsworth.

Dorothy Wordsworth.

William Hazlitt.

Sara Stoddard Hazlitt.

William Godwin.

George Dyer.

Tom Hood.

Bernard Barton.

H. C. Robinson.

Thomas De Quincey.

Allan Cunningham.

W. C. Macready.

### Contemporary English Essayists.

Archibald Alison, 1757–1839.

John Foster, 1770–1843.

Sidney Smith, 1771–1845.

Lord Francis Jeffrey, 1773–1850.

William Hazlitt, 1778–1830.

Lord Henry Brougham, 1779–1868.

Thomas De Quincey, 1785–1859.

Professor John Wilson, 1785–1854.

Thomas Carlyle, 1795–1881.

### Selections from Charles Lamb's Letters to his Friends.

From the Complete Correspondence and Works of Charles Lamb.  1870.

A Poetic Criticism (to Coleridge).  Feb. 13, 1797.

On a Visit to Coleridge (to Manning).  Sept. 24, 1802.

On the Empire of Tartary (to Manning).  Feb. 19, 1803.

On Retiring from the East India House (to Wordsworth). April 6, 1825.

**Selected Books of Reference on Charles Lamb and his Works.**

The Life of Samuel Taylor Coleridge. By James Gillman. 1838.

Biographia Literaria. By S. T. Coleridge. 1842.

Reminiscences of Samuel Taylor Coleridge and Robert Southey. By Joseph Cottle. 1847.

Poems, Life and Letters of Bernard Barton. Edited by his Daughter. 1849.

Recollections of Charles Lamb. By Thomas De Quincey. (De Quincey's Biographical Essays.) 1850.

Recollections of Mary Lamb. By Mary Cowden Clarke. Littell's Living Age. (National Magazine.) April, 1858.

Charles Lamb and Sydney Smith. Atlantic M'thly. Mar., 1859.

The Sad Side of the Humorist's Life. Littell's Living Age. (From the Eclectic Review.) January, 1832.

About Charles Lamb — His Friends and his Books. Dublin University Magazine. 1865.

Charles Lamb: Gleanings after his Biographers. Macmillan's Magazine. April, 1867.

Memoirs of William Hazlitt. 1867.

Diary of H. C. Robinson. 1869.

Lectures on the British Poets. Vol. II., Lect. XIII. By H. Reed. 1870.

Authors at Work: Charles Lamb at his Desk. By C. Pebody. 1872.

Concerning Charles Lamb. Scribner's Magazine. March, 1876.

Elia and Geoffrey Crayon. William Hazlitt's Miscellaneous Works. 1876.

Charles and Mary Lamb (Portrait). By John Buckre. Scribner's Monthly. March, 1881.

Life of Mary Lamb. By Annie Gilchrist. (Famous Women, Series II.) 1883.

Obiter Dicta. By Augustine Birrell. 1887.

# A Guide to the Study of Nineteenth Century Authors.

By LOUISE MANNING HODGKINS,

PROFESSOR OF ENGLISH LITERATURE IN WELLESLEY COLLEGE.

Copyright, 1887.

## WILLIAM WORDSWORTH, 1770-1850.

### Significant Facts in the Life of Wordsworth.

Precocious Imagination.
Education in Cambridge. (Degree, 1792.)
Sympathy with French Revolution.
Poet-Laureate of England. 1843–1850.
Retired Life in Lake Country. 1794–1850.

### Biographical Writings.

Homes and Haunts of British Poets. Vol. II. By William Howitt. 1847.
Life of William Wordsworth. By Christopher Wordsworth. 1851.
Dorothy Wordsworth. A Journal. By J. S. C. Shairp. 1875.
Papers of the Wordsworth Society. 1880.
William Wordsworth. (English Men of Letters Series.) By William Henry Myers. 1881.
The English Lakes and their Genii. By M. D. Conway. Harper's Magazine. February, 1881.

11

Yesterdays with Authors.   (Wordsworth.)   By James T. Fields.   1882.

William Wordsworth.   The Story of his Life.   By James Middleton Sutherland.   1887.

**Wordsworth's Contributions to his own Biography.**

The Prelude.

**A Group of Wordsworth's Literary Friends.**

Dorothy Wordsworth.          Walter Scott.
S. T. Coleridge.              Thomas De Quincey.
Robert Southey.              John Wilson.
Charles Lamb.               Thomas Arnold.

**Selections from Wordsworth.**

LYRICS.

My Heart leaps up.
To the Daisy.
Three Years she grew.
She dwelt among the Untrodden Ways.
She was a Phantom of Delight.
I wandered Lonely as a Cloud.
To the Cuckoo.
The Solitary Reaper.
The Primrose of the Rock.
The Highland Girl.
The Grave of Burns.
The Affliction of Margaret.
Yarrow Unvisited.
Yarrow Visited.
Yarrow Revisited.

**Selected Books of Reference on Wordsworth and his Works.**

Critical Essays. (Famous diatribe.) By Francis Jeffrey. Edinburgh Review. October, 1807–November, 1814.

Biographia Literaria. (Wordsworth.) By Samuel Taylor Coleridge. 1847.

Illustrations of Genius. (Wordsworth.) By Henry Giles. 1850.

Essays on the Poets. (Wordsworth.) By Thomas De Quincey. 1853.

Lectures on Poetical Literature. (Wordsworth.) By D. M. Moir. 1856.

Critical and Miscellaneous Writings. (On Genius and Writings of Wordsworth.) By T. Noon Talfourd. 1856.

Essays : Critical and Imaginative. (Wordsworth.) By Prof. John Wilson. 1856.

Lectures on British Poets. (Wordsworth.) By H. Reed. 1857.

Wordsworth, Shelley, Keats, and Others. (Wordsworth.) By David Masson. 1860. (In North British Review. August, 1850.)

The Works of Wordsworth. By A. H. Clough. North American Review. April, 1865.

Studies in Poetry and Philosophy: Wordsworth, the Man and Poet. By J. S. C. Shairp. 1868.

Yesterdays with Authors. (Wordsworth.) By James T. Fields. 1871.

Theology in the English Poets (Analysis of the Excursion). By Stopford Brooke. 1874.

On Wordsworth. By Walter H. Pater. Fortnightly Review. January–June, 1874.

Wordsworth's Poems. (Introduction.) Edited by A. Grosart. 1875.

Memoir and Letters of Sara Coleridge. By E. Coleridge. 1875.

Essays in Literary Criticism. (Wordsworth and his Genius.) By R. H. Hutton. 1876.

Lectures on Poetry. (Wordsworth.) By Sir F. H. Doyle. 1877.

Poetic Interpretations of Nature. (Wordsworth as Interpreter of Nature.) By J. S. C. Shairp. 1877.

Critical Essays on Poetry. (Wordsworth.) By Sir H. Taylor. 1878.

Studies in Literature (Essays: Wordsworth's Prose; Wordsworth's Relation to the French Revolution; Wordsworth among Idealists). By Edward Dowden. 1878.

The Text of Wordsworth's Poems. By Edward Dowden. Contemporary Review. November, 1878.

Wordsworth. (Introduction to Selected Poems.) By Matthew Arnold. 1879.

Afternoons with the Poets. By Charles D. Deshler. 1879.

Wordsworth. By C. P. Cranch. Atlantic Monthly. February, 1880.

The English Lakes and their Genii. By M. D. Conway. Harper's Magazine. February, 1881.

History of English Thought in the Eighteenth Century. Vol. II. (Wordsworth's Ethics.) By Leslie Stephen. 1881.

Aspects of Poetry. Chapters XI. and XII. By J. S. C Shairp. 1882.

Address to Wordsworth Society. By Matthew Arnold. Macmillan's Magazine. June, 1883.

In Wordsworth's Company. By John Burroughs. The Century. January, 1884.

Wordsworth's Relation to Science. By R. Spence Watson. Macmillan's Magazine. July, 1884.

Wordsworth and Byron.   By C. A. Swinburne.   Nineteenth Century.   April and May, 1884.

Wisdom and Truth of Wordsworth's Poetry.   By Aubrey De Vere.   Catholic World.   March, 1884.

Studies in Wordsworth.   By H. N. Hudson.   1884.

Wordsworth's Passion.   By Titus M. Coan.   New Princeton Review.   May, 1886.

Three Americans and Three Englishmen.   (Wordsworth.)   By C. F. Johnson.   1886.

Essays, chiefly on Poetry.   (Wordsworth.)   By Aubrey De Vere.   1887.

The Prelude.   (An excellent annotated edition.)   By A. J. George.   1888.

# A Guide to the Study of Nineteenth Century Authors.

BY LOUISE MANNING HODGKINS,

PROFESSOR OF ENGLISH LITERATURE IN WELLESLEY COLLEGE.

## THOMAS BABINGTON MACAULAY (LORD MACAULAY), 1800-1859.

### Biographical Writings.

*Chief Biographer of Macaulay*, G. O. TREVELYAN, 1876.

#### Other Contributions to Macaulay's Biography.

A Memoir of Lord Macaulay. By Dean Milman. 1862.
Lord Macaulay : his Life, his Writings. By C. H. Jones. 1880.
Macaulay. By J. Cotter Morison. (English Men of Letters Series.) 1882.

#### A Group of Macaulay's Friends.

| | |
|---|---|
| Hannah More. | Samuel Rogers. |
| Francis Jeffrey. | Thomas Moore. |
| Sidney Smith. | Thomas Campbell. |
| Lady Holland. | Winthrop Mackworth Praed. |

#### Significant Facts in the Life of Macaulay.

Classical and Legal Training (Cambridge, 1822).
Publication of Essay on Milton, 1825.
Admittance to House of Commons, 1830.
Election to the Supreme Council of India, 1834.
Publication of History of England, 1848.

17

### Selected Essays from Macaulay.

| | | |
|---|---|---|
| Milton. | Goldsmith. | Clive. |
| Bacon. | Johnson. | Frederick the |
| Bunyan. | Byron. | Great. |
| Addison. | Dialogue between Milton | Hastings. |
| Dryden. | and Cowley. | |

### Selected Orations from Macaulay.

On Parliamentary Reform.
On the Government of India.
On Copyright.

### Selected Poems from Macaulay.

| | | |
|---|---|---|
| Battle of Ivry. | Horatius. | Virginia. |

### Selected Subjects from Macaulay's History of England.

The Puritans.
Oliver Cromwell.
Society and Manners in the Days of Charles II.
Trial of the Bishops.
Character of William III.
The Revolution of 1688.

### Contemporary English Historians.

William Mitford, 1744–1827.
Alexander Fraser Tytler, 1847–1813.
Henry Hallam, 1777–1859.
Sir William Napier, 1785–1860.
Dean Milman, 1791–1868.
George Grote, 1794–1871.
Thomas Arnold, 1795–1842.
Connop Thirlwall, 1797–1875.

**Selected Books of Reference on Macaulay and his Works.**

Essays Critical and Imaginative. Vol. VII. (Criticism of Lays of Ancient Rome). By Professor Wilson. 1842.

Essays and Reviews. (Macaulay.) By E. P. Whipple. 1843.

A New Spirit of the Age. (Criticism of Macaulay's Essays.) By R. H. Horne. 1844.

Macaulay's History of England. (Unfavorable.) Quarterly Review. December–March, 1848–1849.

The Literati. Vol. III. (Macaulay). (Very unfavorable.) By E. A. Poe. 1850.

Mr. Macaulay as a Politician. (Unfavorable.) Littell's Living Age. August, 1853.

Literary Studies. (Macaulay.) By Walter Bagehot. 1856.

Essays in Biography and Criticism. (Macaulay.) By Peter Bayne. 1858.

Lord Macaulay. By F. D. Maurice. Macmillan's Magazine. February, 1860.

Nil Nisi Bonum. By M. Thackeray. Harper's Magazine. March, 1860.

Lord Macaulay's Place in English Literature. North British Review. August–November, 1860.

Jerrold, Tennyson, and Macaulay. By James H. Stirling. 1860.

Lord Macaulay's Schoolboy. By E. A. Nolan. Macmillan's Magazine. July, 1870.

Authors at Work. (Macaulay.) By C. Pebody. 1872.

Macaulay. By John Morley. Fortnightly Review. April, 1876.

Biographical Sketches. (Macaulay.) By Harriet Martineau. 1876.

Lord Macaulay's Memory. (Littell's Living Age.) (From the Spectator.) May, 1876.

Lord Macaulay. By Edward A. Freeman. International Review. May, 1876.

Review of Trevelyan's Life and Letters of Macaulay. By William E. Gladstone. Quarterly Review. July, 1876.

Lord Macaulay and his Friends. By R. H. Stoddard. Harper's Magazine. June–July, 1876.

Gleanings of Past Years. (Macaulay.) By William E. Gladstone. 1879.

The Tom Side of Macaulay. By D. D. Lloyd. Harper's Magazine. March, 1879.

History of English Thought. (Macaulay.) By Leslie Stephen. 1881.

Macaulay. By Ernest Myers. Frazer's Magazine. February, 1881.

Lord Macaulay, Essayist and Historian. By Albert S. G. Canning. 1882.

Representative British Orations. (Macaulay.) By Charles Kendal Adams. 1884.

# A Guide to the Study of Nineteenth Century Authors.

## By LOUISE MANNING HODGKINS,

PROFESSOR OF ENGLISH LITERATURE IN WELLESLEY COLLEGE.

Copyright, 1887.

## SAMUEL TAYLOR COLERIDGE, 1772-1834.

### Significant Facts in the Life of Coleridge.

Education at Christ's Hospital and Cambridge. (Left without a degree, 1794.)
Friendship with the Wordsworths.
Separation from his Family.
Bondage to the Opium Habit.
Literary Career of Thirty-five Years. 1798–1833.

### Biographical Writings.

Biographia Literaria. By Samuel Taylor Coleridge. 1817.
The Essays of Elia (Christ's Hospital Five and Thirty Years Ago). By Charles Lamb. 1830.
The Life of Samuel Taylor Coleridge. By James Gillman. 1838.
Reminiscences of Coleridge and Southey. By Joseph Cottle. 1847.
Letters from Coleridge to William Godwin. Macmillan's Magazine. April, 1864.
Coleridge. By H. D. Traill. (English Men of Letters Series.) 1884.

### A Group of Contemporary English Poets.

George Crabbe, 1754-1832.
Samuel Rogers, 1763-1855.
William Wordsworth, 1770-1850.
James Hogg, 1770-1835.
Sir Walter Scott, 1771-1832.
Robert Southey, 1774-1843.
Thomas Campbell, 1774-1844.
Thomas Moore, 1779-1852.
Lord Byron, 1788-1824.
Percy Bysshe Shelley, 1792-1822.
John Keble, 1792-1866.
John Keats, 1795-1821.

### Selected Poems from Coleridge.

#### LYRICS.

Kubla Khan.                    The Knight's Tomb.
Love.                          A Day-Dream.
A Christmas Carol.             Youth and Age.
        Answer to a Child's Question.

#### SONNETS.

When British Freedom for a Happier Land.
Thou Gentle Look that didst my Soul beguile.
To the Autumnal Moon.
Dear Native Brook.

#### REFLECTIVE POEMS.

Religious Musings.
Ode to the Departing Year.
France.

Fears in Solitude.
The Lime-Tree Bower my Prison
 (to Charles Lamb).
Frost at Midnight.
Before Sunrise in the Vale of Chamouni.
Dejection. An Ode.

### BALLADS.

The Rime of the Ancient Mariner.
Christabel.
The Ballad of the Dark Ladie.

### DRAMAS.

Selections from Wallenstein. (A Translation from Schiller.)
Selections from Remorse. (First published under the title
of Osorio.)

### Selected Prose from Coleridge.

Seven Lectures on Shakspeare and Milton.
Letters on the Spanish Question. (From The Friend.)
Lay Sermons (Number I.).
Table Talk.

### A Group of Coleridge's Friends.

William Wordsworth.          Thomas De Quincey.
Dorothy Wordsworth.          Edward Irving.
Charles Lamb.                Thomas Wedgwood.
Robert Southey.              Thomas Allsop.
Robert Lovell.               James Gillman.

**Selected Books of Reference on Coleridge and his Works.**

Letters of Robert Southey. Edited by J. W. Warter. 1790–1839.

Letters to Coleridge by Charles Lamb. (In Life and Letters of Charles Lamb.) 1796–1834.

Review of Christabel, Kubla Khan, etc. (For specimen of the early unfavorable reviews.) Edinburgh Review. September, 1816.

Essays on the Lake School of Poetry. (For specimen of the early favorable reviews.) Blackwood's Magazine. October, 1819.

Gallery of Literary Characters. (For portrait.) Fraser's Magazine. July, 1833.

A Review of Coleridge's Poems. (For specimen of an early American review.) North American Review. October, 1834.

Coleridge. (For a specimen of an early review of his philosophy.) Westminster Review. March, 1840.

Coleridge and Opium-Eating. By Thomas De Quincey. Blackwood's Magazine. January, 1845.

Coleridge as a Philosophical Critic. By E. P. Whipple. North American Review. June, 1846.

Literary Reminiscences. (Coleridge.) By Thomas De Quincey. 1851.

Life of William Wordsworth. By Christopher Wordsworth. 1851.

The Life of John Sterling. (Coleridge.) (A matchless word-portrait.) By Thomas Carlyle. 1852.

Lectures on the British Poets. (Coleridge.) By Henry Reed. 1857.

Essays in Biography and Criticism. (Samuel Taylor Coleridge.) By Peter Bayne. 1858.

The Autobiography of Leigh Hunt. (Coleridge.) 1860.

Spiritual Philosophy : founded on the Teaching of the late Samuel T. Coleridge. By Joseph H. Green. 1863.

Diary, Reminiscences, and Correspondence of Henry Crabbe Robinson. Notes on Coleridge. 1869.

A Century of Great Poets from 1750. (Coleridge.) Blackwood's Magazine. November, 1871.

Studies in Poetry and Philosophy. Coleridge : the Man and the Poet. By J. S. C. Shairp. 1872.

Theology in the English Poets. By Stopford Brooke. 1874.

Memoirs and Letters of Sara Coleridge. Edited by her Daughter. 1875.

Lives of Famous Poets. (Coleridge.) By W. M. Rossetti. 1878.

Recollections of Writers. (Coleridge.) By Charles and Mary Cowden Clarke. 1878.

Studies in Literature. (The Transcendental Movement and Literature.) By Edward Dowden. 1878.

Coleridge as Poet and Man. By G. P. Lathrop. Atlantic Monthly. April, 1880.

Essays in Criticism : Joubert. (Comparison of Joubert and Coleridge.) By Matthew Arnold. 1880.

Coleridge, Shelley, and Goethe. By George H. Calvert. 1880.

Retrospect of a Long Life. (Coleridge.) By S. C. Hall. 1883.

Sonnet. (Samuel Taylor Coleridge.) By D. G. Rossetti. 1882.

Samuel Taylor Coleridge and the English Romantic School. By Alois Brandl. 1887.

# A Guide to the Study of Nineteenth Century Authors.

## By LOUISE MANNING HODGKINS,

PROFESSOR OF ENGLISH LITERATURE IN WELLESLEY COLLEGE.

## PERCY BYSSHE SHELLEY, 1792-1822.

### Significant Facts In the Life of Shelley.

Precocious Imagination.
Education at Eton and Oxford. (Expelled from Oxford
1811.)
Vagrant Life in British Isles and Continent.
Domestic Infelicities.
Friendship with Byron and Leigh Hunt.
Residence and Tragic Death in Italy.

### Biographical Writings.

*Chief Biographer of Shelley*, EDWARD DOWDEN, 1886.

#### Other Biographers of Shelley.

Thomas Medwin, 1847.
Thomas Jefferson Hogg, 1858.
Charles S. Middleton, 1858.
William M. Rossetti, 1869.
George Barnet Smith, 1877.
John A. Symonds, 1879.
John Cordy Jeaffreson, 1885.

NOTE.—The most reliable of these biographers are Edward Dowden
and John A. Symonds.

26

Recollections of Byron and some of his Contemporaries. By Leigh Hunt. 1828.

Shelley Papers. By Thomas Medwin. 1832.

Homes and Haunts of the British Poets. By William Howitt. 1857.

Recollections of Shelley and Byron. By E. J. Trelawny. 1858.

Shelley Memorials. Edited by Lady Shelley. 1859.

Shelley. Quarterly Review. October, 1861.

Relics of Shelley. By Richard Garnett. 1862.

On the Drowning of Shelley. By R. H. Horne. Fraser's Magazine. November, 1870.

Shelley's Early Life. By D. F. McCarthy. 1870.

Shelley's Last Days. By Richard Garnett. Fortnightly Review. 1878.

Shelley's Birthplace. By W. H. White. Macmillan's Magazine. March, 1879.

Shelley's Life near Spezzia : his Death and Burial. By H. B. Forman. Macmillan's Magazine. May, 1880.

The Shelley Society Publications. 1886.

**Selections from Shelley contributing to his own Biography.**

Introductory Lines to Alastor.

· Dedication to the Revolt of Islam.

Epipsychidion.

Adonais. Stanzas 31–34.

Hymn to Intellectual Beauty. Stanzas 5 and 6.

Stanzas written in Dejection near Naples.

Letter to Maria Gisborne.

Julian and Maddalo (Shelley and Byron).

## A Group of Shelley's Friends.

Thomas Jefferson Hogg.        William Godwin.
E. J. Trelawny.               Thomas Love Peacock.
Lord Byron.                   Thomas Medwin.
Leigh Hunt.                   Maria Gisborne.
            Mr. and Mrs. Edward Williams.

## Selections from Shelley.

Death and Sleep.   (Introduction to Queen Mab.)
Adonais.   An Elegy on Keats.
Ode to the West Wind.
The Sensitive Plant.
The Cloud.
The Skylark.
" Life of life, thy lips enkindle."   ⎫ Act ii. Sc. 5 ⎫  Prome-
" My soul is an enchanted boat."     ⎭              ⎪    theus
Prometheus' Description of the Cave.  Act iii. Sc. 2 ⎭  Unbound.
Ode to Liberty.
" Music when soft voices die."
Music.
" The world's great age begins anew " (the Last Chorus in
    Hellas).
In the Pine Forest of the Cascine.
To the Nile.   A Sonnet.

## A Tribute of Poets to Shelley.

Memorabilia.   By Robert Browning.
Percy Bysshe Shelley.   By Dante Gabriel Rossetti.
Lerici.   By Aubrey De Vere.
After a Lecture on Shelley.   By Oliver W. Holmes.
Shelley.   By Emily Pfeiffer.

Shelley. By Katharine Lee Bates. In Literary World.
July 1, 1880.
Verses on the Death of P. B. S. By Bernard Barton.
Elegy on the Death of P. B. Shelley. By Arthur Brooke.

### Selected Books of Reference on Shelley and his Works.

Alastor. (An early favorable review of Shelley.) Black-
wood's Magazine. November, 1819.
A New Spirit of the Age. (Mrs. Shelley.) By R. H.
Horne. 1844.
An Introductory Essay to the Letters of Percy Bysshe
Shelley. (Letters : forgeries.) By Robert Browning.
1852.
Essays on the Poets. (Shelley.) By Thomas De Quincey.
1853.
Thoughts on Shelley and Byron. By Charles Kingsley.
Fraser's Magazine. November, 1853.
Literary Studies. By Walter Bagehot. 1856.
Shelley. Westminster Review. 1858.
Autobiography of Leigh Hunt. 1860.
Wordsworth, Shelley, Keats, and others. By David Masson.
1860.
Shelley. In Macmillan's Magazine. May–September, 1860.
Shelley. By Mathilde Blind. Westminster Review. July,
1875.
The Poems of Shelley. (From the North British Review.)
Littell's Living Age. January, 1871.
A Century of Great Poets, from 1750. (Shelley.) Black-
wood's Magazine. April, 1872.
Recollections of Writers. (Shelley.) By Charles and Mary
Cowden Clarke. 1878.
Studies in Literature. (For Shelley's Relation to the French
Revolution.) By Edward Dowden. 1878.

Shelley as a Lyric Poet. (A reasonable discussion of the
defects and beauties of Shelley.) By J. S. C. Shairp.
Fraser's Magazine. July, 1879.
Coleridge, Shelley, Goethe. By G. H. Calvert. 1880.
Shelley : a Study. By John Todhunter. 1880.
Some Thoughts on Shelley. By Stopford A. Brooke.
Macmillan's Magazine. June, 1880.
Literary World. (Shelley.) Aug. 26 and Sept. 23, 1882.
Literary History of England. (Byron, Shelley.) By Mrs.
Oliphant. 1882.
The English Novel. By Sidney Lanier. 1883.
A Leaf from the Real Life of Lord Byron. By J. A.
Froude. Nineteenth Century. August, 1883.
Wordsworth and Byron. By A. C. Swinburne. Nineteenth
Century. April and May, 1884.
Letters to Dead Authors. (Shelley.) By Andrew Lang.
1886.

# A Guide to the Study of Nineteenth Century Authors.

### By LOUISE MANNING HODGKINS,

**PROFESSOR OF ENGLISH LITERATURE IN WELLESLEY COLLEGE.**

Copyright, 1887.

---

## JOHN KEATS, 1795-1821.

### Biographical Writings.

Life, Letters, and Literary Remains of John Keats. By Richard Monckton Milnes (Lord Houghton). 1848.

Life and Poetry of Keats. By David Masson. Macmillan. November, 1860.

On the Vicissitudes of Keats's Fame. By Joseph Severn. Atlantic Monthly. April, 1863.

Recollections of Writers. (Keats.) By Charles and Mary Cowden Clarke. 1878.

The Literary History of England. (Keats.) By Mrs. Oliphant. 1882.

Keats. By Sidney Colvin. (English Men of Letters Series.) 1887.

Keats. By W. M. Rossetti. (Great Writers Series.) 1887

### Significant Facts in the Life of Keats.

Grammar School Education.

Friendship with Charles Cowden Clarke and Leigh Hunt.

Experience in London Hospitals.

Failure of Early Work.     Tragic Death in Rome, 1821.

Publication of Endymion.     Posthumous Fame

## Selections from Keats.

### FROM ENDYMION.

"A Thing of Beauty,"                             Book I.
"At last with sudden step,"                      "   II.
The Palace of Neptune,                           "   III.
"Who, who from Dian's feast would be away,"  "   IV.

### FROM LAMIA.

"She was a Gordian shape," Part I.

### FROM HYPERION.

"As when upon a tranced summer night,"   Book I.
"It was Hyperion,"                               "   II.
"Where was he when the giant of the sun?"  "   III.

### FROM OTHO THE GREAT.

"I should have Orphean lips." — Act v. Scene 5.

The Eve of St. Agnes.
Imitation of Spenser.
Ode to a Nightingale.
Ode on a Grecian Urn.
To Autumn.
Ode on Melancholy.
On first looking into Chapman's Homer.
To Solitude.
Keats's Last Sonnet.
La Belle Dame sans Merci.
Meg Merrilies.
To Mrs. Reynolds's Cat.

**A Tribute of the Poets to Keats.**

Adonais. By P. B. Shelley.
Keats. A Sonnet. By H. W. Longfellow
John Keats. A Sonnet. By D. G. Rossetti.
Keats. A Sonnet. By George L. Moore.
Keats. A Sonnet. By John B. Tabb.

**Selected Books of Reference on Keats and his Works.**

Review of Endymion (thought by some critics to have killed Keats). By William Gifford. (Quarterly Review. April, 1818.

Review of Endymion. (An early favorable review.) By Francis Jeffrey. Edinburgh Review. August, 1820.

Landor's Imaginary Conversations. 1846.

Review of R. M. Milnes's Keats (favorable). Spectator. 1848.

Essays on the Poets. (Keats.) (Unfavorable.) By Thomas De Quincey. 1853.

Wordsworth, Shelley, Keats, and other Essays. By David Masson. 1874.

The Papers of a Critic. (Keats.) By Charles W. Dilke. 1875.

Memoirs and Letters of Sara Coleridge. By her Daughter. pp. 179–182. 1875.

After many Days. (Keats.) By R. H. Stoddard. Scribner's Monthly. January, 1878.

John Keats: a Study. By F. M. Owen. 1880.

Letters and Poems of John Keats. By John G. Speed. 1883.

## A Group of Keats's Friends.

| | |
|---|---|
| Edward Holmes. | Leigh Hunt. |
| Joseph Severn. | J. H. Reynolds. |
| Charles Cowden Clarke. | Benjamin R. Haydon. |
| Charles Armitage Brown. | William Godwin. |
| Basil Montague. | Percy Bysshe Shelley. |

# A Guide to the Study of Nineteenth Century Authors.

By LOUISE MANNING HODGKINS,

PROFESSOR OF ENGLISH LITERATURE IN WELLESLEY COLLEGE.

## LORD BYRON (GEORGE GORDON), 1788-1824.

### Biographies of Byron.

Letters and Journals of Lord Byron. By Thomas Moore. 1830.
Life of Lord Byron. By John Galt. 1830.
Life of Lord Byron. By Friedrich Karl Elze. 1870.
Life of Lord Byron. By Emilio Castelar. (Translated by Mrs. Arthur Arnold.) 1875.
Byron. By John Nichol. (English Men of Letters Series.) 1880.
The Real Lord Byron. By John Cordy Jeaffreson. 1883.

NOTE.—Of these biographers the most unreliable is Moore; the most extravagant, Castelar; the most reasonable, Nichol.

*Other Contributions to Byron's Biography.*

Conversations of Byron. By Thomas Medwin. 1824.
Lord Byron and some of his Contemporaries. By Leigh Hunt. 1828.
Recollections of the Last Days of Shelley and Byron. By E. J. Trelawny. 1858.

### Significant Facts in the Life of Byron.

Unfortunate Youthful Environments.
Education at Harrow and Cambridge.
Publication of Childe Harold.
Profligate Life on the Continent.
Enlistment in Greek Struggle for
Independence.

A poet of whom Byron was ignorant : Spenser.
A poet to whom Byron was indifferent : Shakspeare.
A poet whom Byron admired : Pope.
A poet whom Byron despised : Wordsworth.
A poet whom Byron respected : Shelley.

### A Group of Admirers of Byron.

| | |
|---|---|
| Moore. | Kingsley. |
| Brydges. | Elze. |
| Goethe. | Arnold (Matthew). |
| Scott. | Morris (William). |
| Castelar. | Morley (John). |

### A Group of Censurers of Byron.

| | |
|---|---|
| Jeffrey. | Reed (H.). |
| Lamb. | Thackeray. |
| Southey. | Stowe (H. B.). |
| Landor. | Carlyle. |
| Macaulay. | Moir. |
| Lamartine. | Swinburne. |

### Selections from Byron's Poetry.

#### PERSONAL POEMS.

Stanzas. — "Ah, talk not to me of a name great in story ! "
On a Distant View of Harrow.
On Leaving Newstead Abbey.

"On this Day I complete my Thirty-sixth Year."
Loch Na-Garr.
To Thomas Moore.

### SONNETS.

"Eternal Spirit of the chainless wind."
Two Sonnets to Genevra.

### DRAMAS.

Mont Blanc. (Manfred, Act I. Scene I.)
Death of Manfred. (Manfred, Act III. Scene 4.)
"I speak to Time and to Eternity." (Marino Faliero, Act V.
Scene 3.)

LYRICS.

Isles of Greece.
Maid of Athens.
Fare Thee Well.
The Dream.
" Adieu, adieu, my native land."
(Childe Harold, Canto I. after Stanza 13.)

HEBREW MELODIES.

" She walks in Beauty."
Vision of Belshazzar.
" The Harp the Monarch Minstrel swept."
" Oh, snatched away in Beauty's Bloom ! "
Destruction of Sennacherib.
The Wild Gazelle.

**Selected Books of Reference on Lord Byron and his Works.**

Lord Byron's Poems. (First review of Byron.) Edinburgh Review. January, 1808.

English Bards and Scotch Reviewers. By Lord Byron.
1809.

Review of Manfred. By Lord Jeffrey. Edinburgh Review.
August, 1817.

Childe Harold. (An early American review.) By
W. Phillips. North American Review. May, 1817.

Byron in Greece (presents Byron as a hero and martyr).
Westminster Review. July, 1824.

Letters on Character and Genius of Byron. By Sir Egerton
Brydges. 1825.

Moore's Life of Byron. By W. O. B. Peabody. North
American Review. July, 1830.

Faust, Part II. Act III. (Euphorion, the child of Faust and
Helena, represents Byron.) By Goethe. 1831.
Moore's Life of Lord Byron. By T. B. Macaulay.
Edinburgh Review. 1831.
Byron. By Thomas Carlyle. 1832.
Byron's Dramas. Fraser's Magazine. 1834.
Goethe's Conversations with Eckermann. 1836.
The Works of Lord Byron. By E. P. Whipple. North
American Review. April, 1845.
Lectures and Essays { Moral Philosophy of Byron's Life.
{ Moral Philosophy of Byron's Genius.
By Henry Giles. 1850.
Lectures on Poetical Literature. (Byron.) By D. M. Moir.
1850–51.
Reminiscences. (Byron). By Thomas De Quincey. 1851.
Thoughts about Shelley and Byron. By Charles Kingsley.
Fraser's Magazine. November, 1853.
Lectures on British Poets. (Byron.) By Henry Reed.
1857.
Byron (His relation to the French Revolution). By John
Morley. Fortnightly Review. December, 1870.
Essays in Literary Criticism. (Byron.) By R. H. Hutton.
1876.
Recollections of Writers. By Charles and Mary Cowden
Clarke. 1878.
Studies in Literature. 1789–1877. (Byron's relation to
the French Revolution.) By Edward Dowden. 1878.
Afternoons with the Poets. (Byron's sonnets.) By C. D.
Deshler. 1879.
Modern Greece. (Byron in Greece.) By Richard C. Jebb.
1880.
Introductory Essay to the Poetry of Byron. (Chosen and
arranged by Matthew Arnold.) 1881.

Byron and Wordsworth. By A. C. Swinburne. Nineteenth Century Magazine. April and May, 1884.

Letters to Dead Authors. (Byron.) By Andrew Lang. 1886.

Byron. By William Morris. Encyclopædia Britannica. 1887.

Byron. By C. T. Winchester. Methodist Review. Sept., 1888.

# A Guide to the Study of Nineteenth Century Authors.

### By LOUISE MANNING HODGKINS,

PROFESSOR OF ENGLISH LITERATURE IN WELLESLEY COLLEGE.

---

## WILLIAM MAKEPEACE THACKERAY, 1811-1863.

### Pseudonyms of Thackeray.

| | |
|---|---|
| Michael Angelo Titmarsh. | Ikey Solomon. |
| George Fitzboodle. | Fat Contributor. |
| Charles Jeames Yellowplush. | Manlius Pennialinus. |

### Biographical Writings.

In Memoriam. By Charles Dickens. Cornhill Magazine. March, 1864.

Thackeray, the Humourist and Man of Letters. By John C. Hotten (Theodore Taylor). 1869.

Yesterdays with Authors. (Thackeray.) By James T. Fields. 1873.

William Makepeace Thackeray. By R. H. Stoddard. Harper's Magazine. September, 1874.

Thackeray. By Anthony Trollope. (English Men of Letters Series.) 1879.

Great Novelists. (Thackeray.) By J. C. Watt. 1879.

Thackeray's London. By William H. Rideing. 1885.

Letters of Thackeray (1847-1855). With portrait and reproductions of letters and drawings. 1887.

### Significant Facts in the Life of Thackeray.

Education at Charter House and Cambridge.
Early Artist Life in Weimar and Paris.
Publication of Vanity Fair, 1846.
Lecture Tours in America.
Retired Literary Life in London.

### A Group of Contemporary English Novelists.

Edward George Bulwer Lytton, 1805–1873.
Benjamin Disraeli (Lord Beaconsfield), 1805–1881.
Mrs. E. C. Gaskell, 1810–1865.
Charles Dickens, 1812–1870.
Charles Reade, 1814–1886.
Anthony Trollope, 1815–1882.
Charlotte Brontë, 1816–1855.
Emily Brontë, 1819–1848.
George Eliot, 1820–1880.
William Wilkie Collins, 1824–

### Five Great Novels of Thackeray.

Vanity Fair, 1848.         Henry Esmond, 1852.
Pendennis, 1849.         The Newcomes, 1855.
         The Virginians, 1858.

### Five Minor Works of Thackeray.

The History of Samuel Titmouse and the Great
   Hoggarty Diamond, 1840.
Fitzboodle Confessions, 1843.
English Humourists, 1851.
Book of Snobs, 1851.
Essays on the Four Georges, 1852.

### Selections from the Ballads of Thackeray.

The Ballad of Bouillabaisse.
The King of Brentford's Testament.
The White Squall.
The Mahogany Tree.
The Cane-bottomed Chair.
The Story of the Violet.
Jacob Homnium's Hoss.
Vanitas Vanitatum.

### Periodicals to which Thackeray Contributed.

Punch, 1843–1853.          New Monthly Magazine.
Fraser's Magazine.         Westminster Review.
The National Standard.     Cornhill Magazine.

NOTE. — Thackeray was Editor of the Cornhill Magazine, 1859-1862.

### Books of General Reference.

Preface to Jane Eyre. By Charlotte Brontë. 1847.
Vanity Fair: A Review. Fraser's Magazine. Sept., 1848.
Vanity Fair and Jane Eyre. Quarterly Review. December.
  March, 1848–49.
New Novels. (Esmond.) Fraser's Magazine. Dec., 1852
Thackeray. By George Brimley. Spectator. Nov. 6. 1852.
Thackeray. (A review of Esmond, Pendennis. Barry Lyndon.
  The Snobs.) By J. F. Kirke. North American Review.
  July, 1853.
Thackeray's English Humourists. Littell's Living Age.
  July, 1853.
Mr. Thackeray and his Novels. Blackwood's Magazine.
  January, 1855.
The Newcomes. Quarterly Review. June–September, 1855.

Fielding and Thackeray.   North British Review.   November–February, 1855–56.
Mr. Thackeray's Ballads.   Littell's Living Age.   April, 1856.
Thackeray.   By H. H. Lancaster.   North British Review. March, 1864.
Thackeray.   Westminster Review.   July–October, 1864.
Thackeray.   By Dinah Muloch.   Macmillan's Magazine. February, 1864.
Literary Studies, Vol. II.   (Thackeray.)   By Walter Bagehot. 1864.
William Makepeace Thackeray.   By Bayard Taylor.   Atlantic Monthly.   March, 1864
The Style of Balzac and Thackeray.   Littell's Living Age. January, 1865.
Studies on Thackeray.   By James Hannay.   1869.
Thackeray and Sterne.   Littell's Living Age.   January, 1870.
Recollections of William Makepeace Thackeray.   By George Hodder.   Harper's Magazine.   July, 1870.
Haud Immemor.   Thackeray in America.   By W. B. Reed Blackwood's Magazine.   June, 1872.
The Best of All Good Company.   By Blanchard Jerrold.   1874.
Poets and Novelists.   (Thackeray.)   By George B. Smith. 1876.
Mr. Thackeray's Sketches.   Blackwood's Magazine.   February, 1876.
Thackeray as a Draughtsman.   By Russell Sturgis.   Scribner's Magazine.   June, 1880.
Thackeray's Relation to English Society.   By E. S. Nadal. Scribner's Magazine.   February, 1881.
Letters to Dead Authors.   (Thackeray.)   By Andrew Lang. 1886.

# A Guide to the Study of Nineteenth Century Authors.

By LOUISE MANNING HODGKINS,

PROFESSOR OF ENGLISH LITERATURE IN WELLESLEY COLLEGE

Copyright, 1887.

## CHARLES DICKENS, 1812-1870.

### Significant Facts in the Life of Dickens.

Early Street Education.
Boy Reporter.
Publication of Sketches by Boz.
Publication of Pickwick Papers.
Visits to America.
Sustained Popularity.

### Biographical Writings.

Charles Dickens ; The Story of his Life. By John C. Hottei (Theodore Taylor). 1870.

Footprints of Charles Dickens. By M. D. Conway. Har per's Magazine. September, 1870.

In Memoriam. By "A. H." Macmillan's Magazine. May–July, 1870.

The Life of Charles Dickens. By John Forster. 1871.

The Best of All Good Company. (A Day with Charles Dickens.) By Blanchard Jerrold. 1872.

Charles Dickens and Rochester. By Robert Langton. 1880.

45

The Letters of Charles Dickens, edited by his Sister-in-Law and Eldest Daughter. 1880.
Dickens. By A. W. Ward. (English Men of Letters Series.) 1882.
Recreations of a Literary Man : Charles Dickens at Home. By Percy Fitzgerald. 1883.

### Occupations of Dickens.

Newspaper Reporter.
Sketch-writer.
Novelist.
Editor.

Public Reader.
Historian.
Poet.
Writer and Actor of Dramas.

### A Group of Dickens's Friends.

John Forster.
Walter Savage Landor.
Thomas Carlyle.
Lord Houghton (Richard
   Monckton Milnes).
Douglas Jerrold.
H. K. Browne (Phiz).
Wilkie Collins.
Henry W. Longfellow.

Daniel Maclise (Clarkson
   Stanfield).
W. C. Macready.
Charles Fechter.
Mark Lemon.
Lord Lytton (Edward
   Bulwer).
James T. Fields.
Mary Cowden Clarke.

### Twelve Best Works of Charles Dickens.

Pickwick Papers.
Oliver Twist.
Nicholas Nickleby.
Old Curiosity Shop.
Martin Chuzzlewit.
Dombey and Son.

David Copperfield.
Bleak House.
Little Dorrit.
A Tale of Two Cities.
Great Expectations.
Our Mutual Friend.

NOTE. — Number of novels written by Charles Dickens, 16. Date of publication, 1837–1870.

**Selections from Dickens's Poems.**

The Ivy Green.
A Christmas Carol.
The Hymn of the Wiltshire Labourers.
Child's Hymn.

**Selections from Dickens's Dramas.**

The Strange Gentleman.     The Village Coquette.

**A Critical Essay by Charles Dickens**

On Mr. Fechter's Acting.

**Selected Books of Reference on Charles Dickens and his
Works.**

Dickens in France. By W. M. Thackeray. 1842.
Charles Dickens. By C. C. Felton. North American
Review. January, 1843.
A New Spirit of the Age. Charles Dickens. By R. H.
Horne. 1844.
Novels and Novelists. By E. P. Whipple. North American
Review. October, 1849.
Charles Dickens and David Copperfield. Fraser's Magazine.
December, 1850.
Dickens's " Bleak House." By George Brimley. From The
Spectator. 1853.
Remonstrances with Dickens. Blackwood's Magazine.
April, 1857.
Literary Studies. By Walter Bagehot. 1858.
A Visit to Charles Dickens. By Hans Christian Andersen.
Eclectic Magazine. May–August, 1864.
Modern Novelists. (Charles Dickens.) Westminster Review
July–October, 1864.

The Genius of Dickens.   Atlantic Monthly.   May, 1867.

Modern Men of Letters.   (Dickens.)   By J. H. Friswell.
1870.

Yesterdays with Authors.   By James T. Fields.   1871.

Recollections of Writers.   By Charles and Mary Cowden
Clarke.   1878.

Charles Dickens's Verse.   Littell's Living Age.   January,
1878.

Review of Charles Dickens.   By W. Minto.   Fortnightly
Review.   July–December, 1879.

Great Novelists.   (Dickens.)   By James Crabb Watt.   1880.

About England with Dickens.   By Editor Scribner's Monthly.
August, 1880.

In London with Dickens.   By B. E. Martin.   Scribner's
Monthly.   March, 1881.

Plays and Poems of Charles Dickens.   By R. H. Shepherd.
1882.

Recreations of a Literary Man.   Charles Dickens as an
Editor.   By Percy Fitzgerald.   1883.

Letters to Dead Authors.   (Dickens.)   By Andrew Lang.
1886.

# A Guide to the Study of Nineteenth Century Authors.

By LOUISE MANNING HODGKINS,

PROFESSOR OF ENGLISH LITERATURE IN WELLESLEY COLLEGE.

Copyright, 1887.

## ELIZABETH BARRETT BROWNING, 1806-1861.

### Significant Facts in the Life of Mrs. Browning.

Classical Education.
Early Invalid Life.
Marriage to Robert Browning, 1846.
Residence in Florence, Italy, 1846–1861.

### Biographical Writings.

A New Spirit of the Age. (E. B. Barrett.) By R. H. Horne. 1844.

Elizabeth Barrett Browning. By Kate Field. Atlantic Monthly. September, 1861.

The Late Elizabeth Barrett Browning. Littell's Living Age. July–September, 1861.

Life, Letters, and Essays of Elizabeth Barrett Browning. (Letters addressed to R. H. Horne. Preface and Memoir. By R. H. Stoddard.) 1877.

### Selections from Mrs. Browning.

#### *Lyrics.*

The Sea Men.  
A Vision of Poets.  
The Cry of the Children.  
Rhyme of the Duchess May.  
Lady Geraldine's Courtship.  
The Dead Pan.  
Night and the Merry Man.  

Confessions.  
Lay of the Brown Rosary.  
My Doves.  
Cowper's Grave.  
My Heart and I.  
Bertha in the Lane.  
The Sleep.  

#### *Sonnets.*

The Soul's Expression.  
Tears.  
Comfort.  
Work.  

Cheerfulness Taught by  
Reason.  
The Prospect.  
To Hugh Stuart Boyd.  
(Legacies.)  

#### *From the Portuguese Sonnets.*

" I thought once how Theocritus had sung."  
" Go from me."  
" What can I give thee back ? "  
" If thou must love me."  
" I never gave a lock of hair away."  
" I lived with visions for my company."  
" First time he kissed me."  
" How do I love thee ? "  

#### *Selections from Aurora Leigh.*

" I think I see my father's sister stand."  Book 1.  
" I had a little chamber in the house."  " 1.  
" My own best poets."  " 1.  
" Times followed one another.  Came a morn  
I stood upon the brink of twenty years."  " 11.

### Criticisms upon Mrs. Browning's Aurora Leigh.

Mrs. Barrett Browning : Aurora Leigh.  Blackwood's Maga-
zine.  January, 1857.
Aurora Leigh.  Westminster Review.  October, 1857.
Elizabeth Barrett Browning.  British Quarterly Review.
May, 1862.
Elizabeth Barrett Browning.  Eclectic Magazine.  October,
1862.

### Poems illustrating Mrs. Browning's Love of Italy.

Casa Guidi Windows.          A Court Lady.
Napoleon III. in Italy.      Mother and Poet.
    Italy and the World.

### Dramatic Selections.

" Eternity stands always fronting God." }    From
" Is it thy voice ? "                    } A Drama of Exile.

### Selections from Mrs. Browning's Translations.

Psyche and Pan.  (From Metamorphoses.)  ·
Hector and Andromache.  (From the Iliad.)
Ode to the Swallow.  (From Anacreon.)
Prometheus Bound.  (From Æschylus.)

### Mrs. Browning's Prose.

The Greek Christian Poets.    The Book of the Poets.

### Poems of Elizabeth Barrett Browning contributing to her own Biography.

The Lost Bower.            To Flush, my Dog.
The Deserted Garden.       Sonnets to H. S. Boyd.
Hector in the Garden.      Wine of Cyprus.
            Sonnets from the Portuguese.

### Poems of Robert Browning alluding to Elizabeth Barrett Browning.

One Word More.            Oh, Lyric Love.  (From The
At the Fireside.           Ring and the Book.)
Prospice.

### Selected Books of Reference on Mrs. Browning and her Works.

A New Spirit of the Age.  (E. B. Barrett.)  By R. H.
Horne.  1844.

Poems of Elizabeth Barrett Barrett.  Blackwood.  November, 1844.

Recollections of a Literary Life.  Married Poets.  By Mary
Russell Mitford.  1852.

Poems by Elizabeth Barrett Browning.  North American
Review.  February, 1857.

Poems by Elizabeth Barrett Browning. By C. C. Everett.
North American Review. October, 1857.

The Works of Elizabeth Barrett Browning. Edinburgh
Review. October, 1861.

Elizabeth Barrett Browning. (An interpretation of Mrs.
Browning's Napoleonic sympathies.) By E. D. Macmillan's Magazine. September, 1861.

Mrs. Browning. British Quarterly Review. July–October,
1861.

Elizabeth Barrett Browning. By C. B. Conant. North
American Review. April, 1862.

Last Poems and other Works of Mrs. Browning. North
British Review. May, 1862.

Elizabeth Barrett Browning. Eclectic Magazine. March,
1862.

English Poets in Italy. (Mrs. Browning's last poems.) By
A. Wilson. Macmillan's Magazine. May, 1862.

Elizabeth Barrett Browning. By E. C. Stedman. Scribner's
Monthly. November, 1873.

Poets and Novelists. (Elizabeth Barrett Browning.) By
George Barnet Smith. 1875.

Memoirs and Letters of Sara Coleridge. (To John Kenyon
on Miss Barrett, 1844 ; to Ellis Yarnall on Mrs. Browning,
1851.) Edited by her Daughter. 1875.

Mrs. Browning's Letters to R. H. Horne. By H. James, Jr.
Nation. February, 1877.

English Poetesses : Elizabeth Barrett Browning. By Eric
S. Robertson. 1883.

# A Guide to the Study of Nineteenth Century Authors.

## By LOUISE MANNING HODGKINS,

PROFESSOR OF ENGLISH LITERATURE IN WELLESLEY COLLEGE.

Copyright, 1887.

---

## ROBERT BROWNING, 1812-.

### Significant Facts in the Life of Robert Browning.

Education in London University and Italy.
Publication of Paracelsus, 1835.
Marriage with Elizabeth Barrett Barrett, 1846.
Death of Mrs. Browning, 1861.
Publication of the Ring and the Book, 1869.

### Biographical Writings.

A New Spirit of the Age. By R. H. Horne. 1844.
Life and Letters of Mrs. Browning. (Containing a description of Robert Browning.) By R. H. Horne. 1877.
Italian Note-Books. (" A London Breakfast " and " A Visit to Casa Guidi.") By Nathaniel Hawthorne. 1880.
A Handbook to the Works of Robert Browning. By Mrs. Sutherland Orr. 1885.
Introduction to W. J. Rolfe's and H. E Hersey's Select Poems. 1886.
Browning Society Papers.

**Selections from the Shorter Lyric and Dramatic Poems of Browning.**

Evelyn Hope.
The Pied Piper of Hamelin.
Up at a Villa.
A Toccata of Galuppi's.
By the Fireside.
Saul.
A Grammarian's Funeral.
One Word More.
Home Thoughts from Abroad.
The Englishman in Italy.
The Last Ride Together.
Oh, Lyric Love. (From The Ring and the Book.)
Gold Hair.
Prospice.
Clive.
Hervé Riel.
Andrea del Sarto.
The Bishop orders his Tomb.

Two in the Campagna.
How they Brought the Good News from Ghent to Aix.
The Boy and the Angel.
Meeting at Night.
Parting at Morning.
My Last Duchess.
The Lost Leader.
Memorabilia.
Wanting is — What?
The Flight of the Duchess.
Amphibian.
Old Pictures in Florence.
Fra Lippo Lippi.
Rabbi Ben Ezra.
An Epistle containing the Strange Medical Experience of Karshish, an Arab Physician.
Abt Vogler.

**Selected Dramas.**

Pippa Passes, 1841.
A Blot in the 'Scutcheon, 1843.

Colombe's Birthday, 1844.
Luria, 1845.
A Soul's Tragedy, 1845.

**Browning's Greatest Dramatic Poem.**

The Ring and the Book, 1869.

**Selections from Hellenic Poems.**

Pheidippides.                    Agamemnon,
Balaustion's Adventure.

**Selected Books of General Reference on Robert Browning.**

Browning.  British Quarterly Review.  1847.
Bells and Pomegranates.  By J. R. Lowell.  North American Review.  April, 1848.
Christmas Eve and Easter Day.  Littell's Living Age.  May, 1850.
Men and Women.  British Quarterly Review.  January-April, 1856.
Robert Browning.  Review of Men and Women, Sordello, Strafford, etc.  Putnam's Magazine.  April, 1855.
The Poems and Plays of Robert Browning.  North American Review.  May, 1861.
Robert Browning's Poems.  Edinburgh Review.  October, 1864.
Wordsworth, Tennyson, and Browning ; or, Pure, Ornate, and Grotesque Art in English Poetry.  By Walter Bagehot.  National Review.  November, 1864.
Mr. Browning's Sordello.  By Edward Dowden.  Fraser's Magazine.  October, 1867.
The Ring and the Book.  By John Addington Symonds.  Macmillan's Magazine.  November–April, 1868–1869.
On the Ring and the Book.  By John Morley.  Fortnightly Review.  January–June, 1869.
The Ring and The Book.  Edinburgh Review  July, 1869.
James Russell Lowell and Robert Browning.  New Englander.  January. 1870.
Our Living Poets.  (Browning.)  By H. Buxton Forman.  1871.
Browning's Poems.  Littell's Living Age.  January, 1871.
Balaustion's Adventure.  Edinburgh Review.  January. 1871.
The Ring and the Book.  Littell's Living Age.  March, 1871.

Balaustion's Adventure. By Sidney Colvin. Fortnightly
Review. July–December, 1871.
Browning as a Preacher. By E. D. West. Littell's Living
Age. December, 1871.
The Red Cotton Night-cap Country By J. R. Dennett.
The Nation. August, 1873.
Robert Browning. By Edmund C. Stedman. Scribner's
Monthly. December, 1874.
Victorian Poets. (Robert Browning.) By E. C. Stedman.
1876.
Stories from Browning. By Mrs. Sutherland Orr. 1882.
Robert Browning. By Roden Noel. Littell's Living Age.
December, 1873.
A Handbook to the Works of Robert Browning. By Mrs.
Sutherland Orr. 1885.
An Introduction to the Study of Robert Browning's Poetry.
By Hiram Corson. 1886.
The Pre-Raphaelite Brotherhood. By W. Holman Hunt.
Contemporary Review. April–May, 1886.
Studies in Literature. Mr. Tennyson and Mr. Browning.
A Comparative Study. By Edward Dowden. 1886.
Select Poems of Robert Browning. By W. J. Rolfe and
H. E. Hersey. 1886.
Christmas Eve and Easter Day. By H. E. Hersey. 1886.
An Introduction to the Study of Browning. By Arthur
Symonds. 1886.
A Blot in the 'Scutcheon. Edited by W. J. Rolfe and
H. E. Hersey. 1887.
Studies in the Poetry of Robert Browning. By James
Fotheringham. 1887.
The Spiritual Element in Robert Browning's Poetry. By
Hamilton Wright Mabie. Andover Review. August, 1887.

# A Guide to the Study of Nineteenth Century Authors.

BY LOUISE MANNING HODGKINS,

PROFESSOR OF ENGLISH LITERATURE IN WELLESLEY COLLEGE.

Copyright, 1888.

---

## ALFRED (LORD) TENNYSON, 1809-    .

### Significant Facts in the Life of Alfred Tennyson.

Early Life in Lincolnshire.
Education at Trinity College, Cambridge.
Friendship with Arthur Hallam.
Publication of his Earlier Poems, 1829 and 1832.
Laureateship, 1850.
D. C. L. of Oxford, 1859.
Elevation to the Peerage, 1884.
Retired Life at the Isle of Wight.

### Biographical Writings.

A New Spirit of the Age. By R. H. Horne. 1844.
Homes and Haunts of the most Eminent British Poets.
By William Howitt. 1847.
Lincolnshire Scenery and Character, as illustrated by Mr.
Tennyson.    By a Lincolnshire Rector.    Macmillan's
Magazine.    November–April, 1873–74.
Tennysoniana.    1879.
Alfred Tennyson: his Life and Works.    By W. E. Wace.
1881.

The Borderlands of Surrey. By Alice Maude Fenn. Century Magazine, August, 1882.
Alfred, Lord Tennyson. A Biographical Sketch. By H. J. Jennings. 1884.
A Biographical Sketch. By Anne Thackeray Ritchie. (Introduction to Harper's Edition, 1884.)
The Young People's Tennyson. (Introduction to Notes.) By W. J. Rolfe. 1886.

### Selections from Tennyson's Early Poems.

*(Before 1842.)*

The Poet.
The Deserted House.
The Merman.
The Mermaid.
The Lady of Shalott.
The Two Voices.

The Miller's Daughter.
Œnone.
The Lotos-Eaters.
A Dream of Fair Women.
The Blackbird.
The Death of the Old Year.

### Selections from Tennyson's Later Poems.

*(After 1842.)*

Morte d'Arthur.
Tithonus.
Locksley Hall.
St. Agnes' Eve.
" Move eastward, happy Earth."
The Charge of the Light Brigade.
" Flower in the Crannied Wall."
The Coming of Arthur.
The Holy Grail.
The Passing of Arthur.
Rizpah.
In the Children's Hospital.

To-morrow.
Early Spring.
Locksley Hall — Sixty Years After.
The Brook.
The Grandmother.
The Revenge : A Ballad of the Fleet.

### In Memoriam.

"Strong Son of God, immortal Love,"        I.
"To sleep I give my powers away,"          IV.
"Calm is the morn without a sound,"        XI.
" I envy not in any moods,"                XXVII.
"With trembling fingers did we weave,"     XXX.
" Her eyes are homes of silent prayer,"    XXXII.
"Could we forget the widowed hour,"        XL..
" How fares it with the happy dead ? "     XLIV.
" Be near me when my light is low,"        L..
"Oh, yet we trust that somehow good,"      LIV.
"The wish, that of the living whole,"      LV.
" 'So careful of the type?' but no,"       LVI.
" The truth came borne with bier and pall," LXXXV.
" I past beside the reverend walls,"       LXXXVII
" You say, but with no touch of scorn,"    XCVI.
" Ring out, wild bells, to the wild sky,"  CVI.
" Now fades the last long streak of snow," CXV.
" Love is and was my Lord and King,"       CXXVI.
" O true and tried, so well and long,"     CXXXI.

### A Study of Portraits from Tennyson.

The Lady of Shalott.
A Dream of Fair Women.
The Gardener's Daughter.
St. Simeon Stylites.

The Sleeping Beauty.
Sir Galahad.
Sir Launcelot and Queen Guinevere.
The Coming of Arthur.   (Arthur.)
Gareth and Lynette.   (Lynette.)
Geraint and Enid.   (Geraint.)          From
Merlin and Vivien.   (Vivien.)      The Idylls of
Launcelot and Elaine.   (Elaine.)      the King.
The Passing of Arthur.   (Arthur.)

### Selected Songs from Tennyson's Longer Poems.

"As through the land at eve we went."   (The Princess.)
"Sweet and low."   (The Princess.)
"Tears, idle tears."   (The Princess.)
"Home they brought her warrior dead."   (The Princess.)
"Ask me no more."   (The Princess.)
"Go not, happy day."   (Maud.)
"Come into the garden. Maud."   (Maud.)
"I come from haunts of coot and hern."   (The Brook.)
"Low, lute, low!"   (Queen Mary.)
"Two young lovers, in winter weather."   (Harold.)

### Comparison of Tennyson with Other Poets.

English Poets of the Nineteenth Century.   By E. P.
  Whipple.   North American Review.   July, 1845.
Keats and Tennyson : Conversations with the Poets.   By
  J. R. Lowell.   1846.
Sketches of the Poetical Literature of the Past Half-Century.
  By D. M. Moir.   1851.
Ruskin on the Ancient and the Modern Poets.   Homer and
  Tennyson.   By J. O. S.   Fraser's Magazine.   June, 1856.
Literary Studies : Wordsworth, Tennyson, and Browning.
  By Walter Bagehot.   National Review.   November, 1864.

Jerrold, Tennyson, and Macaulay. By J. H. Sterling. 1868.
Yesterdays with Authors. By James T. Fields. 1871.
Tennyson and Theocritus. By E. C. Stedman. Atlantic
Monthly. November, 1871.
Virgil and Tennyson. By a Lincolnshire Rector. Mac-
millan's Magazine. November, 1875.
Studies in Literature: Mr. Tennyson and Mr. Browning.
By Edward Dowden, 1878.
Sketches of Eminent Statesmen. (Byron and Tennyson.)
By A. Hayward, 1880.
Tennyson and Musset. By A. C. Swinburne. Fortnightly
Review. February, 1881.

### Selected Books of Reference on Alfred Tennyson and his Works.

Tennyson's Poems. (An early favorable criticism.) West-
minster Review. January–April, 1831.
On Some of the Characteristics of Modern Poetry, and on
the Lyrical Poems of Alfred Tennyson. By Arthur Henry
Hallam. The English Magazine. August, 1831.
Tennyson's Poems. (An unfavorable review of early poems.)
By Professor John Wilson. Blackwood's Magazine. 1832.
Tennyson's Poems. (The earliest American review.) By
John S. Dwight. Christian Examiner. 1863.
Review of Tennyson's Poems. By John Sterling. 1842.
Tennyson's Princess. Edinburgh Review. July–October.
1849.
Tennyson. By Charles Kingsley. Fraser's Magazine. Sep-
tember, 1850.
In Memoriam. Westminster Review. October. 1850.
Tennyson's Princess. By Gerald Massey. Christian So-
cialist, a Journal of Association. September–November,
1851.

Tennyson's Maud. (For analysis of Maud.) Fraser's Magazine. September, 1855.

Maud. (An unfavorable criticism.) Blackwood's Magazine. September, 1855.

Maud, and other Poems. (For Tennyson's peculiarities of versification.) British Quarterly Review. July-October, 1855.

Essays : Tennyson's Poems. By George Brimley. 1855.

Tennyson and his Poetry. By Gerald Massey. 1855.

Tennyson's Maud Vindicated : The Spirit and Purpose of Maud. By Robert James Mann, M.D. 1856.

Idylls of the King. British Quarterly Review. July-October, 1859.

The Poetical Character : illustrated from the Works of Alfred Tennyson, D.C.L., Poet Laureate. By Rev. Alfred Gatty. December, 1859.

Mr. Tennyson, and the Idylls of King Arthur. By G. B. Bacon. New Englander. February, 1860.

Mr. Tennyson's Felicitous Changes. By A. K. H. Boyd. Fraser's Magazine. February, 1863.

The Two Voices. By Mrs. C. R. Corson. New Englander, October, 1863.

Mr. Tennyson's Northern Farmer. By J. M. Ludlow. Macmillan's Magazine. May-October, 1864.

Enoch Arden. Blackwood's Magazine. November, 1864.

"Tears, Idle Tears." A commentary. By George Grove. Macmillan's Magazine. November-April, 1866-67.

The Arthurian Legend in Tennyson. By S. Cheetham. Contemporary Review. January-April, 1868.

On Mr. Tennyson's Lucretius. By R. C. Jebb. Macmillan's Magazine. June, 1868.

A Study of the Works of Alfred Tennyson. By E. C. Tanish, 1868.

A Concordance to the Entire Works of Alfred Tennyson. By D. Baron Brightwell. 1869.

The Idylls of the King. By Henry Alford. Contemporary Review. January, 1870.

The Epic of Arthur. Edinburgh Review. January–April, 1870.

The Songs of the Wrens. By H. R. Haweis. The St. Paul's Magazine. February, 1871.

Mr. Tennyson as a Botanist. By J. Hutchinson. The St. St. Paul's Magazine. October–December, 1873.

History of English Literature. By H. A. Taine. (Tennyson.) 1874.

Mr. Tennyson's Social Philosophy. By Lionel Tollemache. Fortnightly Review. February, 1874.

Analysis of Mr. Tennyson's In Memoriam. By F. W. Robertson. 1875.

Tennyson's Queen Mary. (A favorable criticism, classing it above Browning's dramas.) Quarterly Review. July–October, 1875.

Essays in Literary Criticism. (Tennyson.) By R. H. Hutton. 1876.

Victorian Poets. (Tennyson.) By Edmund Clarence Stedman. 1876.

Queen Mary. Harold. (An unfavorable criticism.) Edinburgh Review. January–April, 1877.

Critical Essays. (Tennyson.) By Bayard Taylor. 1877.

A Tennysonian Retrospect. By J. S. Ward. Atlantic Monthly. September, 1879.

Tennysoniana. By R. H. Shepherd. 1879.

Lessons from my Masters. (Tennyson.) By Peter Bayne 1879.

Gleanings of Past Years. (Tennyson.) By W. E. Gladstone. 1879.

A New Study of Tennyson. Parts I. and II. By J. C. C.
Littell's Living Age. July–September, 1880.

Tennyson's Poems. British Quarterly Review. October,
1880.

A Study of Tennyson. By R. H. Stoddard. North-
American Review. July, 1881.

Aspects of Poetry. By J. S. C. Shairp. 1882.

A Key to Tennyson's In Memoriam. By Alfred Gatty, D.D.
1882.

Tennyson's Dream of Fair Women, and Two Voices. By
Professor Corson. 1882.

The Princess. Edited by W. J. Rolfe. 1883.

Select Poems from Tennyson. Edited by W. J. Rolfe. 1884.

Tennyson's In Memoriam: its Purpose and its Structure.
A Study. By J. F. Genung. 1884.

Tennyson's Last Volume. By T. H. S. Escott. Fortnightly
Review. January–June, 1886.

The Young People's Tennyson. Edited by W. J. Rolfe.
1886.

Poets and Problems. (Tennyson.) By George Willis Cooke.
1886.

Dethroning Tennyson. A Contribution to the Tennyson-
Darwin Controversy. By A. C. Swinburne. Nineteenth
Century. January, 1888.

# A Guide to the Study of Nineteenth Century Authors.

BY LOUISE MANNING HODGKINS,

PROFESSOR OF ENGLISH LITERATURE IN WELLESLEY COLLEGE.

Copyright, 1888.

---

## DANTE GABRIEL ROSSETTI, 1828-1882.

### Significant Facts in the Life of Dante Gabriel Rossetti.

Admission to Ford Madox Brown's studio.
Union with the Pre-Raphaelite Brotherhood.
Connection with the Germ (called afterwards Art and Poetry).
Marriage to Elizabeth Eleanor Siddall.
Death of his wife.
Residence in Cheyne Walk, Chelsea.
Publication of first volume of poems.

### Biographical Writings.

Recollections of Dante Gabriel Rossetti. By T. Hall Caine. 1882.

Dante Gabriel Rossetti : a Record and Study. By William Sharp. 1882.

Dante Gabriel Rossetti : his Work and Influence, including a Brief Survey of Recent Art Tendencies. By William Tirebuck. 1882.

66

Dante Gabriel Rossetti. By Mary A. Robinson. Harper's Magazine. October, 1882.
Dante Gabriel Rossetti. (With portraits.) By E. W. Gosse. Century. 1882.
The Truth about Rossetti. By Theodore Watts. Nineteenth Century. March, 1883.
Memorials of Rossetti. Atlantic Monthly. 1883.
Dante Gabriel Rossetti, Poet and Painter. By P. W. Nicholson. (Round Table Series.) 1886.
Life of Dante Gabriel Rossetti. By Joseph Knight. (Great Writers' Series.) 1887.

### A Group of Rossetti's Friends.

| | |
|---|---|
| Ford Madox Brown. | Robert Browning. |
| Oliver Madox Brown. | William Morris. |
| William Bell Scott. | E. Burne Jones. |
| John Ruskin. | A. C. Swinburne. |
| J. E. Millais. | Canon Dixon. |
| Theodore Watts. | Philip Bourke Marston. |
| Frederick Shields. | T. Hall Caine |
| Alfred Tennyson. | William Sharp. |

William Morris.

### The Original Pre-Raphaelite Brotherhood.

| | |
|---|---|
| D. G. Rossetti. | Thomas Woolner. |
| J. E. Millais. | James Collinson. |
| Holman Hunt. | F. G. Stephens. |

W. M. Rossetti.

### Later Pre-Raphaelites.

| | |
|---|---|
| A. C. Swinburne. | William Morris. |

E. Burne Jones.

**Selections from Rossetti.**

### LYRICS.

The Blessed Damozel.     The Woodspurge.
The Burden of Nineveh.     A Young Firwood.
Dante at Verona.     Honeysuckle.
The Portrait.     The Sea Limits.
My Sister's Sleep.     The Cloud Confines.
Love Lily.     " Alas, so Long."
Penumbra.     The Carillon.

### BALLADS.

Troy Town.     The White Ship.
Sister Helen.     The King's Tragedy.

### SONNETS ON LIFE.

Love Enthroned.     Soul Light.
Bridal Birth.     Venus Victrix.
Heart's Hope.     Severed Selves.
Silent Noon.     Willow Wood.

### SONNETS ON CHANGE AND FATE.

Inclusiveness.     A Dark Day.
Lost Days.

### SONNETS ON PICTURES.

The Wine of Circe.     Sibylla Palmifera.
Mary Magdalene.     Fiammetta.

### SONNETS ON THE POETS.

William Blake.     John Keats.
Samuel Taylor Coleridge.     Percy Bysshe Shelley.

### SONNETS ON NATURE.

Winter.                          Spring.
           Autumn Idleness.

### TRANSLATIONS.

Beauty. (From Sappho.)
Francesca da Rimini. (From Dante.)
Viva Nuova. (From Dante.)

### Selections from Rossetti's Prose.

The Stealthy School of Criticism. Athenæum. Dec. 16, 1871.
Hand and Soul. Fortnightly Review. December, 1870.

### Books of General Reference.

The Growth of Early Italian Poetry. The National Review. July–October, 1862.

Rossetti's Poems. (A charge of sensualism.) By J. R. Dennett. North American Review. November, 1870.

The Poems of Dante Gabriel Rossetti. By John Skelton (Shirley). Fraser's Magazine. May, 1870.

The Poems of Dante Gabriel Rossetti. By Algernon Charles Swinburne. Fortnightly Review. January–June, 1870.

Dante Gabriel Rossetti : Painter and Poet. By W. J. Stillman. Putnam's Magazine. 1870.

Our Living Poets. (Rossetti.) By Harry Buxton Forman. 1871.

The Poetical Writings of Mr. Dante Gabriel Rossetti. Westminster Review. January–April, 1871.

Victorian Poets. (Dante Gabriel Rossetti.) By Edmund Clarence Stedman. 1876.

The Poetry of Rossetti. British Quarterly Review. July to October, 1882.

Æsthetic Poetry. By J. S. C. Shairp. Contemporary Review. July, 1882.

New Poetry of the Rossettis and Others. Atlantic Monthly. January, 1882.

The Æsthete. By Frederic Harrison. Pall-Mall Gazette. May, 1882.

Modern Essayists. (Rossetti and the Religion of Beauty.) By F. W. H. Myers. 1883.

Ward's English Poets. (Rossetti.) By W. H. Pater. 1883.

The Art of Rossetti. (A defence of Rossetti against the charge of sensualism.) By Harry Quilter. Contemporary Review. January, 1883.

The Painted Poetry of Watts and Rossetti. By Mrs. E. I. Barrington. Nineteenth Century. June, 1883.

Boston Herald. July 2, 1883.

English Pre-Raphaelite School of Painters. By Helen B. Merriman. Andover Review. 1884.

Anne Gilchrist: her Life and Writings. By Herbert Harlakenden Gilchrist. 1887.

# A Guide to the Study of Nineteenth Century Authors.

## BY LOUISE MANNING HODGKINS,

PROFESSOR OF ENGLISH LITERATURE IN WELLESLEY COLLEGE.

---

## GEORGE ELIOT, 1819-1880.

By birth, Mary Ann Evans.
By *nom de plume*, George Eliot.
By choice, Mrs. George Henry Lewes.
By marriage, Mrs. John Walter Cross.

**Significant Facts in the Life of George Eliot.**

Early life in Warwickshire.
Private education.
Translation of Strauss's Life of Jesus.
The death of her father, Robert Evans.
First journey to the Continent.
Early life in London, and connection with the
Westminster Review.
Influence of Herbert Spencer.
Union with George H. Lewes.
Publication of Adam Bede.
Marriage to John Walter Cross.

## Biographical Writings.

*Chief Biographer of George Eliot,* JOHN WALTER CROSS, 1884.

English Authors in Florence. By Kate Field. Atlantic Monthly. December, 1864.

George Eliot. By Frederic W. H. Myers. (For a good portrait.) Century Magazine. November, 1881.

George Eliot : a Critical Study of her Life. Writings, and Philosophy.[1] By George Willis Cooke. 1884.

George Eliot's Life. By Henry James, Jr. Atlantic Monthly. May, 1885.

The Life of George Eliot. By Frederic Harrison. Fortnightly Review. March, 1885.

Scenes from the George Eliot Country. By S. Parkinson. 1888.

Number of works written by George Eliot, 15, — translations, 2 ; sketches and essays, 2 ; poems, 3 ; novels, 8.

### Selected Novels.

Adam Bede.                    Romola.
The Mill on the Floss.        Middlemarch.
Silas Marner.                 Daniel Deronda.

### Selections from Essays and Reviews.

German Wit. Heinrich Heine. Westminster Review. January, 1856.

Worldliness and Other Worldliness. (The Poet Young.)

Carlyle's Life of John Sterling. Westminster Review. January, 1852.

---

[1] The best general analysis of the life, character, and works of George Eliot.

### Selections from Poems of George Eliot.

How Lisa loved the King.
Stradivarius.
"Oh, may I join the Choir Invisible!"

FROM THE SPANISH GYPSY.

"The time is great, and greater no man's trust.
. . . And long of limb,"                                    Book I.
" 'Tis daylight still, . . . in a long farewell,"       "      I.
Juan's Song: " Day is dying,"                          "      I.
"Why, it is magical! . . . Into the darkness
painfully,"                                                     "      I.
"So soft a night was never made for sleep, . . .
blare of day,"                                                 "      I.
Pablo's Song: "The world is great,"               "      II.
"Let men contemn us, . . . rotten-seeming seed,"   "   III.
Fedelma's Prayer: "Father, my soul is weak,"      "   III.

### Selected Books of Reference on George Eliot and her Works.

GEORGE ELIOT COMPARED WITH OTHER AUTHORS.

George Eliot and Hawthorne. North British Review. August–November, 1860.
Elsie Venner and Silas Marner. By J. M. Ludlow. Macmillan's Magazine. May–October, 1861.
Thomas Carlyle and George Eliot. By James Bryce. The Nation. March 24, 1881.
George Eliot and Emerson. The Century Magazine. February, 1882.
Thackeray and George Eliot. By M. L. Henry. Atlantic Monthly. February, 1883.

George Eliot and Thomas Carlyle.  By Stopford Brooke.
The Independent.  March 24, 1883.
The Rustic of George Eliot and Thomas Hardy.  Merry
England.  May, 1883.

DISCUSSION OF THE NOVELS OF GEORGE ELIOT.

Scenes of Clerical Life.  Atlantic Monthly.  May, 1858.
A New Novelist.  Saturday Review.  July, 1858.
Adam Bede.  Westminster Review.  January and April,
 1859.
Adam Bede.  Blackwood's Magazine.  April, 1859.
Adam Bede.  Atlantic Monthly.  October, 1859.
The Mill on the Floss.  Blackwood's Magazine.  May,
 1860.
The Mill on the Floss.  Westminster Review.  July, 1860.
To Novelists, and a Novelist.  Macmillan's Magazine.
 November–April.  1860–61.
Romola.  Westminster Review.  July and October, 1863.
Felix Holt.  Contemporary Review.  September–December,
 1866.
Felix Holt, the Radical.  By A. G. Sedgwick.  North
 American Review.  October, 1866.
Middlemarch.  Quarterly Review.  January and April, 1873.
Middlemarch.  By Sydney Colvin.  Fortnightly Review.
 January–June.  1873.
Middlemarch.  By T. S. Perry.  North American Review.
 April, 1873.
Two Cities.  Two Books.  Blackwood's Magazine.  July,
 1874.
Daniel Deronda.  By A. V. Dicey.  The Nation.  Oct. 12
 and 19, 1876.
Daniel Deronda.  By Sydney Colvin.  Fortnightly Review.
 November, 1876.

Daniel Deronda: a Conversation. By Henry James, Jr.
Atlantic Monthly. December, 1876.
Middlemarch and Daniel Deronda. By Edward Dowden.
Contemporary Review. December–May, 1876–77.
Daniel Deronda. By Edwin C. Whipple. North American
Review. January, 1877.
Impressions of Theophrastus Such. By G. E. Woodbury.
The Nation. June 19, 1879.

### DISCUSSION OF CHARACTERS FROM GEORGE ELIOT.

George Eliot's Novels. By John Morley. Macmillan's
Magazine. May–October, 1866.
George Eliot's Heroines. Spectator. March, 1876.
Mordecai. (Daniel Deronda.) By Joseph Jacobs. Mac-
millan's Magazine. May–October, 1877.
George Eliot's Children. By Annie Matheson. Macmillan's
Magazine. October, 1882.
George Eliot and her Heroines. By Abba Goold Woolson.
1886.

### DISCUSSION OF THE POETRY OF GEORGE ELIOT.

George Eliot as a Poet. By Matthew Brown (W. B.
Rands). Contemporary Review. May–August, 1868.
The Spanish Gypsy. By John Morley. Macmillan's Maga-
zine. July, 1868.
Poetry and George Eliot. By Shirley (John Skelton).
Fraser's Magazine. July–December, 1868.
Our Living Poets. (George Eliot's Poetry.) By Harry
Buxton Forman. 1871.
Poems of George Eliot. By W. D. Howells. Atlantic
Monthly. July, 1874.

The Legend of Jubal and other Poems by George Eliot.
By Henry James, Jr. North American Review. October, 1874.
English Poetesses. (George Eliot.) By Eric Robertson.
1883.

### Selected Books of General Reference on George Eliot and her Works.

George Eliot's Novels. By H. H. Lancaster. North British
Review. September–December. 1866.
George Eliot and George Lewes. By Justin McCarthy.
The Galaxy. June, 1869.
A Free Lance in the Field of Life and Letters. By W. C.
Wilkinson. 1874.
Essays in Literary Criticism. (George Eliot.) By R. H.
Hutton. 1876.
George Eliot and Comtism. London Quarterly Review.
October and January. 1876–77.
George Eliot as a Novelist. Westminster Review. July and
October, 1878.
George Eliot. By Francis Maguire, Jr. International
Review. July, 1879.
The Ethics of George Eliot's Works. By John Crombie
Brown. 1881.
George Eliot and the Novel. By Edward Eggleston. The
Critic. Jan. 15, 1881.
George Eliot: a General Review. Cornell Magazine. Jan-
uary–March, 1881.
The Village Life of George Eliot. Fraser's Magazine.
February, 1881.
George Eliot. Blackwood's Magazine. February, 1881.
The Moral Influence of George Eliot. By One who Knew
her. Contemporary Review. February, 1881.

George Eliot. By Leslie Stephen. Littell's Living Age. March, 1881.

George Eliot. By C. Kegan Paul. Harper's Magazine. May, 1881.

George Eliot. (A Character Study, by a Personal Friend.) By Edith Simcox. Nineteenth Century Magazine. May, 1881.

George Eliot's Life and Writings. By W. Fraser Rae. International Review. May and June, 1881.

Fiction Fair and Foul. By John Ruskin. Nineteenth Century Magazine. October, 1881.

George Eliot. London Quarterly Review. October and January, 1881 and 1882.

George Eliot. Famous Women Series. By Mathilde Blind. 1883.

The English Novel, and the Principle of its Development. By Sidney Lanier. 1883.

Modern Guide of English Thought in Matters of Faith. (George Eliot as an author.) By R. H. Hutton. 1887.

Essays and Reviews of George Eliot. (Introductory Essay.) By Mrs. S. B. Herrick. 1887.

# A Guide to the Study of Nineteenth Century Authors.

## BY LOUISE MANNING HODGKINS,

PROFESSOR OF ENGLISH LITERATURE IN WELLESLEY COLLEGE.

---

## THOMAS CARLYLE, 1795-1881.

### Significant Facts in the Life of Carlyle.

Scotch and Puritan parentage.
Education at Edinburgh University.   (Without degree.)
Early studies in German literature.
Marriage to Jane Welsh.
Life at Craigenputtock.
Publication of Sartor Resartus.
Literary life in London (Chelsea).
Lord Rector of Edinburgh University.

NOTE. — Carlyle's active literary career extends from the publication of Sartor Resartus, 1831, to the completion of Frederick the Great, 1865.

### Biographical Writings.

*Chief Biographer of Carlyle,* JAMES ANTHONY FROUDE.

English Traits.   (Carlyle.)   By Ralph Waldo Emerson. 1856.

Thomas Carlyle.   By James Grant Wilson.   Harper's Magazine.   April, 1874.

Thomas Carlyle, Philosophical Thinker, Theologian, Historian, and Poet.   By Edwin Paxton Hood.   1875.

78

Thomas Carlyle: his Life, his Books, his Theory. By
Alfred S. Guernsey. 1879.
Thomas Carlyle. By Mrs. Oliphant. Macmillan's Maga-
zine. April, 1881.
Carlyle's Laugh. By Thomas Wentworth Higginson.
Atlantic Monthly. October, 1881.
The Early Days of Thomas Carlyle. By James Anthony
Froude. Nineteenth Century. July, 1881.
Life and Writings of Thomas Carlyle. By R. H. Shepherd.
1881.
Thomas Carlyle: the Man and his Book. By W. H. Wylie.
1881.

### Famous Residents of Cheyne Walk, Chelsea, and its Neighborhood.

Tobias Smollett.  
Joseph M. W. Turner.  
Daniel Maclise.  
Leigh Hunt.  
Mrs. Senior.  
Thomas Carlyle.

Frances Power Cobbe.  
William Bell Scott.  
M. Planché.  
Mrs. Somerville.  
Dante Gabriel Rossetti.  
George Eliot.

### A Group of Carlyle's Friends.

Edward Irving.  
Ralph Waldo Emerson.  
Johann Wolfgang von Goethe.  
Francis Jeffrey.  
John Sterling.  
Thomas Cooper.  
Mrs. Austen.  
Leigh Hunt.  
Arthur Hugh Clough.

Walter Savage Landor.  
Henry Taylor.  
John Ruskin.  
Sir Robert Peel.  
Mazzini.  
James Anthony Froude.  
Lord and Lady Ashburton.  
John Forster.  
David Masson.

NOTE. -- Most eminent disciple of Carlyle, John Ruskin.

### Positions of Carlyle in Literature and Life.

Translator.                Prose poet.
Essayist.                  Orator.
Historian.                 Conversationist.
Biographer.                Moral and religious teacher.
                Censor of his age.

### Selections from Studies in German Literature.

#### TRANSLATIONS.

Wilhelm Meister.   (Criticism of Hamlet.)

#### ESSAYS.

Jean Paul Friedrich Richter.
Nibelungen Lied.
Goethe.

### Selections from Carlyle.

#### SARTOR RESARTUS.

Reminiscences.
The World in Clothes.        Book I.
The World out of Clothes,      "   I.
The Everlasting No,           "   II.
The Everlasting Yea,          "   II.
Church Clothes.               "   III.
Natural Supernaturalism,       "   III.

#### HEROES AND HERO-WORSHIP.

The Hero as Poet.   (Shakspeare.)
The Hero as Man of Letters.   (Johnson and Burns.)
The Hero as King.   (Cromwell.)

CHARTISM.

The Word Impossible.

ORATIONS.

On the Choice of Books. (Inaugural Address at Edinburgh. 1866.)

PAST AND PRESENT.

The Sphinx.                    Gospel of Mammonism.
Hero Worship.                  Labour.
Monk Samson.                   Reward.

LATTER-DAY PAMPHLETS.

The Year 1848.
A Prison Thirty Years Ago.

HISTORICAL WORKS.

Meaning of the French Revolution. (Terror, Book IV.,
vol. 1.)
Battle of Dunbar. (Letters and Speeches of Oliver
Cromwell.)
Portraits of Frederick the Great and of Frederick William.
(Frederick the Great.)
On History. (Miscellaneous Essays.)

BIOGRAPHICAL WORKS.

The Life of John Sterling. (Chapters: Coleridge; Not
Curate.)
Life of Schiller. (Kant's Philosophy.)

## MISCELLANIES.

The Diamond Necklace. { Affinities.
{ Missa est.
Sir Walter Scott.
Characteristics.
Death of Edward Irving.
Shooting Niagara : and after?

### Selections from the Poems of Carlyle.

Tragedy of the Night Moth.
The Sower's Song.
To-day.
Drummwhinn Bridge

### Selected Works on the Philosophy of Carlyle.

Carlyle : Mirage Philosophy. Blackwood's Magazine. 1859
History of English Literature. By H. A. Taine. Vol. IV.,
    Chapter : Philosophy and History. (Carlyle.)   1864.
Three Great Teachers of our own Time.   By Alex. H.
    Japp.   1865.
Carlyle. By John Morley. Fortnightly Review. July. 1870.
Recent British Philosophy. By David Masson.   1875.
Lessons from my Masters.   By Peter Bayne.   Chap. XIII.
    1879.
Essays Philosophical and Theological.   By J. Martineau.
    1879.
The Philosophy of Carlyle.   By Edwin D. Mead.   1881.
Ethics of Carlyle.   By Leslie Stephen.   Cornhill Magazine.
    1881.
Modern Guide of English Thought in Matters of Faith.
    By R. H. Hutton.   1887.

**Selected Books of Reference on Thomas Carlyle and his Works.**

Thomas Carlyle. (An early favorable review of Sartor Resartus.) By A. H. Everett. North American Review. October, 1835.

Miscellanies. (Carlyle.) By Harriet Martineau. 1836.

Carlyle's Works. (A review of The French Revolution.) Dublin Review. October, 1838.

Review of Letters and Speeches of Oliver Cromwell. North British Review. November–February, 1845–46.

Lectures and Essays. (Carlyle.) By Henry Giles. 1850.

Writings and Opinions of Thomas Carlyle. (Carlyle and his American Imitators.) By Mr. Field. New Englander. February, 1850.

Carlyle's Life of Sterling. By George Eliot. Westminster Review. January, 1852.

Carlyle's Theology. By James Martineau. National Review. October, 1856.

Thomas Carlyle. By G. S. Phillips. Atlantic Monthly. December, 1857.

Essays. (Carlyle's Life of Sterling.) By George Brimley 1860.

Essayists, Old and New. North British Review. August–November, 1862.

A Letter to Thomas Carlyle. By David A. Wasson. Atlantic Monthly. October, 1863.

Mr. Carlyle. (A review of Frederick the Great.) Fraser's Magazine. December, 1865.

Lectures and Essays. (Comparison of Milton and Carlyle.) Lecture IV. By J. R. Seeley. 1870.

My Study Windows. (Carlyle.) By James Russell Lowell. 1871.

Mr. Carlyle on Verse. Littell's Living Age. (From the Spectator.) Feb. 11, 1871.

Essays and Reviews. (Thomas Carlyle as a Politician.) By Edwin P. Whipple. 1871.

Memoirs and Letters of Sara Coleridge. (On Heroes and Hero Worship.) Edited by her Daughter. 1875.

Mr. Carlyle's Anthology. By Edward Barrett. 1876.

Studies in Literature. 1789–1877. (The Transcendental Movement.) By Edward Dowden. 1878.

Lessons from my Masters. (Carlyle.) By Peter Bayne. 1879.

A Study of Carlyle. By the author of The Moral Influence of George Eliot. Contemporary Review. January–June, 1881.

Reminiscences. By Sir Henry Taylor. Nineteenth Century Magazine. June, 1881.

Carlyle's Political Influence. By E. L. Godkin. Nation. April 28, 1881.

Thomas Carlyle and George Eliot. By J. Bryce. The Nation. March 24, 1881.

Thomas Carlyle. (Carlyle's Relation to Humanity.) By J. D. Sedgwick. The Nation. Feb. 17, 1881.

A Conversation with Carlyle. By William Knighton. Contemporary Review. January–June, 1881.

Mr. Carlyle's Reminiscences. By Andrew Lang. Fraser's Magazine. April, 1881.

Memories of Old Friends. By Caroline Fox. 1882.

Aspects of Poetry. (Prose Poets.) By J. S. C. Shairp. 1882.

Carlyle and Emerson. Atlantic Monthly. April, 1883.

George Eliot and Carlyle. By Stopford Brooke. Independent. March 24, 1883.

Arnold on Emerson and Carlyle. By John Burroughs. The Century Magazine. 1884.

Another Word on Carlyle. By John Burroughs. The Critic Nov. 29, 1884.

Obiter Dicta. (Carlyle.) By Augustine Birrell. 1884.

Carlyle in London. Atlantic Monthly. March, 1885.

Froude's Life of Carlyle. By Frederick Harrison North. American Review. January, 1885.

Discourses in America. (Emerson.) By Matthew Arnold. 1885.

Carlyle as seen in his Works. By James Kerr. 1887.

Reminiscences. By Thomas Carlyle. Edited by Charles Eliot Norton. 1887.

# A Guide to the Study of Nineteenth Century Authors.

## By LOUISE MANNING HODGKINS,

PROFESSOR OF ENGLISH LITERATURE IN WELLESLEY COLLEGE.

Copyright, 1889.

--- --- --- --- ---

## JOHN RUSKIN. 1819-.

### Significant Facts in the Life of Ruskin.

Birth in London.
Early Religious Teachings.
Early Impressions from Nature, *e.g.*, Visit to Friar's Crag.
Early Tory Predilections.
Education at Christ Church, Oxford. 1836–1840.
Publication of First Volume of Modern Painters. 1843.
Friendship with Thomas Carlyle.
Vindication of Turner as a Landscapist.
The Sale, on Ethical Grounds, of his Bank of England Stock.
Professor of Art at Oxford. 1869–1876.
Foundation of St. George's Guild. 1871.
Frequent Sojourns in Italy.
Retired Life in the English Lake Region.

NOTE. — Mr. Ruskin's present home is Brantwood, near Coniston, Westmoreland.

## Biographical Writings.

### CHIEF CONTRIBUTION TO THE BIOGRAPHY OF RUSKIN.

Preterita : Scenes of my Past Life.   By John Ruskin.
1886–1887.

### OTHER CONTRIBUTIONS TO THE BIOGRAPHY OF RUSKIN.

The Beauties of Ruskin.   (Introduction.)   By L. C. Tuthill.   1859.

The Queen of the Air.   (Preface.)   By John Ruskin.   1871.

Fors Clavigera.   By John Ruskin.   1871–1878.

Lessons from my Masters.   (Ruskin.)   By Peter Bayne.
1879.

Pen Pictures of Modern Authors.   (Ruskin.)   By William
Shepard.   1882.

Life and Teaching of John Ruskin.   By J. Marshall Mather.
1883.

A Conversation with Ruskin.   The Christian Union.   (From
the Pall Mall Gazette.)   May 22, 1884.

### A Group of Contemporary English Art Critics.

John Ruskin.

W. H. Hunt.

J. E. Millais.

Professor Hodgson.

Professor Church.

P. G. Hammerton.

S. Redgrave.

G. F. Watts.

J. W. Mollett.

A. C. Carr.

William Morris.

J. P. Richter.

E. T. Pointer.

F. M. Brown.

F. Wedmore.

F. W. Moody.

### Selected Characteristic Works of Ruskin.

From Ruskin's First Period.   1834–1843.
Modern Painters.   Vol. I.

# JOHN RUSKIN.

From Ruskin's Second Period.  1843–1860.
Modern Painters.  Vol. II.  1846.
Seven Lamps of Architecture.  1849.
Poems.  Published in 1850.  (Written from Early Youth.)
The King of the Golden River.  (A Wise Tale for Children.)  1851.
The Stones of Venice.  Vol. II.  1851–1853.
Edinburgh Lectures on Architecture and Painting.  1853.

From Ruskin's Third Period.  1860–.
Modern Painters.  Vol. V.  1856.
Sesame and Lilies.  1864–1865.
The Ethics of the Dust.  1866.
Aratra Pentelici.  1872.
Saint Mark's Rest.  1877.

NOTE. — Ruskin has published between thirty and forty works, which treat of the following general themes; Art, Architecture, Nature, Poetry, Fiction, Political Economy, Education, Religion.  His greatest work is Modern Painters.

### Selections from the Poetry of Ruskin.

The Last Smile.              Charitie.
Christ Church, Oxford.       The Hills of Carrara.
The Old Water-Wheel.        A Walk in Chamouni.

### Selections from the Prose of Ruskin.

#### BOOKS FOR YOUNG PEOPLE.

The King of the Golden River : or, the Black Brothers.
The Ethics of the Dust.  (Simple Expositions of the Laws of Crystallization.)

#### READING.

Sesame and Lilies.  Lectures I. and II.

## EDUCATION.

Public Education Irrespective of Class-distinction.
Time and Tide.   Letter 16.
Higher Education.   Modern Painters.   Vol. III., Part IV.,
Chap. V., § 6.
Education.   General.   Modern Painters.   Vol. III., Part
IV., Chap. XVII.

## NATURE.

A Snow-Drift.   Modern Painters.   Vol. I., Part II., Sect. IV.,
Chap. II., § 19.
A Mud-Puddle.   Modern Painters.   Vol. I., Part II., Sect.
V., Chap. I., § 4.
The Grass.   Modern Painters.   Vol. III., Part IV., Chap.
XIV., §§ 49-53.
Modern Landscape.   (The Supremacy of Scott.)   Modern
Painters.   Vol. III., Part IV., Chap. XVI., §§ 30-45.
A Stone.   Modern Painters.   Vol. IV., Part V., Chap. XVIII.,
§ 7.
Earth, a Fit Home for Man.   Modern Painters.   Vol. V.,
Part VI., Chap. I., § 3.
The Pine Tree.   Modern Painters.   Vol. V., Part VI.,
Chap. IX., §§ 6-11.
The Character and Mission of Flowers.   Modern Painters.
Vol. V., Part VI., Chap. X., § 7.
The Lichens and Mosses.   Modern Painters.   Vol. V.,
Part VI., Chap. X.. §§ 24 and 25.
Clouds.   (The Angel of the Sea.)   Modern Painters.   Vol.
V., Part VII., Chap. IV.
An Olive Tree.   The Stones of Venice.   Vol. III., Period
III., Chap. IV., §§ 14-20.
The Sky.   Modern Painters.   Vol. I., Part II., Sect. III..
Chap. I.

Mountains. Modern Painters. Vol. I., Part II., Sect. IV., Chaps. I. and II.

NOTE. — Frondes Agrestes is a good selection of readings from Modern Painters.

## DESCRIPTIVE PASSAGES.

The Trient. Modern Painters. Vol. IV., Part V., Chap. XIX., § 3.

Nuremberg. Modern Painters. Vol. V., Part IX., Chap. IV., §§ 6–8.

The Thames below London Bridge. Modern Painters. Vol. V., Part IX., Chap. IX., § 8.

Venice. Stones of Venice. Vol. I., Chap. XXI., § 9, and Vol. II., Chap. I., §§ 1 and 2.

Latrator Anubis. St. Mark's Rest. Chap. II.

## CHARACTER DELINEATION.

Arthur Burgess. The Century Guild. Vol. II. 1887.

## DRAWING AND PAINTING.

Truth of Color. Modern Painters. Vol. I., Part II., Sect. II., Chap. II.

Turner's Slave Ship. Modern Painters. Vol. I., Part II., Sect. V., Chap. III., §§ 29–40.

Idealism in Humanity, as shown by the Old Masters. Modern Painters. Vol. II., Part III., Sect. I., Chap. XIV., §§ 13–15.

Imagination Contemplative. Modern Painters. Vol. II., Part III., Sect. II., Chap. III.

The Real Nature of Greatness of Style. Modern Painters. Vol. III., Part IV., Chap. III.

The True Ideal. Modern Painters, Vol. III., Part IV., Chap. VII.

The Use of Pictures.    Modern Painters.    Vol. III., Part
IV., Chap. X.

Qualifications of the Painter.    Modern Painters.    Vol. V.,
Part VIII., Chap. IV., §§ 20–23.

Claude and Poussin.    Modern Painters.    Vol. V., Part IX.,
Chap. V.

Pre-Raphaelitism.    (A Defence of the Pre-Raphaelite School
in general and Turner in special.)

The Hercules of Camarina.    (The Use of the Greek in Art,
a Lecture before an Art School.)    The Queen of the Air.

The Three Divisions of the Art of Painting.    The Laws of
Fésole.    Chap. II.

### ARCHITECTURE.

The Lamp of Truth.    (Ornament.)    The Seven Lamps of
Architecture.    Chap. II., §§ 5–19.

The Lamp of Beauty.    (Giotto's Campanile at Florence.)
Seven Lamps of Architecture.    Chap. IV., § 43.

The Lamp of Life.    (Ornament.)    Seven Lamps of Architecture.    Chap. V., § 24.

St. Mark's.    Stones of Venice.    Vol. II., Period I., Chap. IV.

The Nature of the Gothic.    Stones of Venice.    Vol. II.,
Period II., Chap. VI.

The Grotesque.    Stones of Venice.    Vol. III., Period III.,
Chap. III., §§ 70–75.

The Mountain Cottage.    (Switzerland.)    The Poetry of
Architecture.    The Cottage.    III.

The British Villa.    The Poetry of Architecture.    The Villa.
IV. and V.

### IMAGINATION.

Power and Office of Imagination.    Modern Painters.
Vol. II., Part III., Sect. II., Chaps. I.–IV.

The Imagination in Scripture.    Aratra Pentelici.    Lecture III.

The Influence of Imagination in Architecture.    The Two
Paths.    Lecture IV.

ETHICS AND RELIGION.

Typical Beauty. Modern Painters. Vol. II., Part III., Sect. I., Chap. XI.
Man, the Image of God. Modern Painters. Vol. V., Part IX., Chap. I., §§ 10–15.
The Contemplation of Evil by the Greek and Christian. Modern Painters. Vol. V., Part IX., Chap. III., §§ 7–9.
Kindness a Sign of High Breeding. Modern Painters. Vol. V., Part IX., Chap. VII., §§ 7 and 8.
The Practical Result of Infidelity. Modern Painters. Vol. V., Part IX., Chap. XII., § 9.
The Death of Moses. Frondes Agrestes. Sect. IX., § 90.
The Pride of Science. Stones of Venice. Vol. III., Period III., Chap. II., §§ 28–32.
Infidelity. Stones of Venice. Vol. III., Period III., Chap. II., §§ 93–103.
Play. Stones of Venice. Vol. III., Period III., Chap. III., §§ 24–32.
Work. (By the Tests of Honesty, Usefulness, and Cheerfulness.) The Crown of Wild Olive. Lecture I.
The Construction of Sheepfolds. (An Essay on Church Government.)
The Relation of Art to Morals. Lectures on Art. Lecture III. (Oxford Lectures of 1870.)

POLITICAL ECONOMY.

The Veins of Wealth. Unto This Last. Essay II.
Mastership. Munera Pulveris. Chap. VI.
Accumulation and Distribution. The Political Economy of Art. Lecture II.

NOTE.—The prose selections in this leaflet are made from the edition of John Wiley & Son. New York. 1875.

**Selected Books of Reference on Ruskin and his Works.**

Modern Painters. Blackwood's Magazine. October, 1843
(A Criticism of Ruskin's Position on Turner.)
Modern Painters. Frazer's Magazine. March, 1846.
The Seven Lamps of Architecture. North American
Review. April, 1851.
The Stones of Venice. North British Review. February--
August, 1854.
Modern Painters. Quarterly Review. March, 1856.
Ruskinism. By G. F. Chorley. Edinburgh Review. April,
1856.
The True and the Beautiful. (Selections from the Works of
Ruskin up to 1858.) Edited by Mrs. L. C. Tuthill. 1859.
The Elements of Drawing. Blackwood's Magazine. Janu-
ary, 1860. (A criticism on Ruskin's theory of drawing.)
Modern Painters. British Quarterly Review. October, 1860.
Mr. Ruskin at the Sea-Side: A Vacation Medley. By
Shirley (John Skelton). Frazer's Magazine. 1860.
The Writings of Mr. Ruskin. North British Review.
February, 1862.
The Critical Character. Westminster Review. October,
1863.
Three Great Teachers of Our Time. (Carlyle, Tennyson.
and Ruskin.) By Alex. H. Jabb. 1865.
Precious Thoughts. Moral and Religious. (Selections from
Ruskin's Works.) Edited by Mrs. L. C. Tuthill. 1866.
Sesame and Lilies. By R. Sturgis, Jr. North American
Review. January, 1866.
Ruskin's New Lectures on Art. By H. N. Day. New
Englander. October, 1870.
Ruskin's Political Economy. By W. J. Stillman. The
Nation. March 30. 1871.

Modern Leaders. (Ruskin.) By Justin McCarthy. 1872.

Art Culture. (Selected from Works of Ruskin.) By W. H. Platt. 1873.

Mr. Ruskin's Recent Writings. By Leslie Stephen. Frazer's Magazine. June, 1874.

Essays. (The Writings of John Ruskin.) By H. H. Lancaster. 1876.

Mr. Ruskin's Letter to Young Girls. Littell's Living Age. (From The Spectator.) January 6, 1877.

Mr. Ruskin's Will. Littell's Living Age. (From The Spectator.) May 12, 1877.

Microscopic Extravagance. Littell's Living Age. May 12, 1877.

Lessons from My Masters. (Carlyle, Tennyson, Ruskin.) By Peter Bayne. 1879.

Belcaro. (Ruskinism.) By Vernon Lee (Violet Paget). 1881.

Ruskin's Arrows of the Chace. By A. G. Sedgwick. The Nation. September 15, 1881.

Aspects of the Thought and Teaching of John Ruskin. By Edmund J. Baillie. 1882.

John Ruskin; Economist. By Patrick Geddes. Round Table. Series III. 1884.

John Ruskin. By W. J. Stillman. Century. January, 1888.

The Work of John Ruskin. By Dr. Charles Waldstein. Harper's Magazine. February, 1889.

NOTE. — Bibliographies of Ruskin have been issued by R. H. Shepherd, 1878, and by W. S. Kennedy in the Literary World, Vol. 16, p. 205. 1885.

# A Guide to the Study of Nineteenth Century Authors.

By LOUISE MANNING HODGKINS.

PROFESSOR OF ENGLISH LITERATURE IN WELLESLEY COLLEGE.

---

## MATTHEW ARNOLD, 1822-1888.

### Significant Facts in the Life of Matthew Arnold.

The Son of Arnold of Rugby.

Winner of Newdigate Prize at Oxford. 1843.*

Friendship with Arthur Hugh Clough.

Publication of "The Strayed Reveller and Other Poems by A." 1849.†

The Professorship of Poetry at Oxford. 1857–1867.

Honorary Degrees of LL.D. Edinburgh, 1869; Oxford, 1870; Cambridge, 1880.

Foreign Missions in Behalf of Education. 1859–1860, 1865, 1885.

NOTE.—No biography of Arnold has yet been published. An excellent sketch of his life may be found under Books of Reference. Pall Mall Gazette. April 19, 1888.

---

* Dean Stanley and Ruskin were winners of the Newdigate Prize.

† Number of works published by Arnold is twenty. The dividing line between Arnold's poetic and prose career may be placed at the time of his resignation of his chair at Oxford. Arnold was an essayist a poet, an educationalist, and a theological writer.

## A Group of Contemporary Literary Critics.

| *English.* | *American.* |
|---|---|
| 1. Matthew Arnold. | 1. E. P. Whipple. |
| 2. J. H. Newman. | 2. J. R. Lowell. |
| 3. R. H. Hutton. | 3. G. W. Curtis. |
| 4. Andrew Lang. | 4. E. C. Stedman. |
| 5. A. C. Swinburne. | 5. H. W. Mabie. |

## Selections from the Poetry of Matthew Arnold.

### NARRATIVE.

Sohrab and Rustum.

*Selections :*

1. " But Rustum strode to his tent door."
2. " He spoke and Rustum answered not."
3. " As when some hunter in the Spring had found."
4. " Truth sits upon the lips of dying men."

Saint Brandon.
The Neckan.
The Forsaken Merman.

### ELEGIAC.

Requiescat.
The Scholar Gypsy.
Thyrsis.
A Southern Night.

Haworth Churchyard.
Rugby Chapel.
Obermann Once More.

### DRAMATIC.

Stagirius.
Tristram and Iseult.
Fragment of an " Antigone."

Philomela.
Empedocles on Etna, Act I.,
Scene 2.

LYRIC.

A Memory Picture.              Dover Beach.
Resignation.                   Self Dependence.
"Yes! in the sea of life       Morality.
  enisled."                     A Summer Night.
The Terrace at Berne.          The Buried Life.
Calais Sands.                   A Wish.

SONNETS.

Quiet Work.                    The Rachel Group.
Shakespeare.                   East London.
To a Republican Friend.        West London.
  1848.                        Monica's Last Prayer.

Selections from the Prose of Arnold.

CLASSICAL.

Celtic Literature.   Parts IV. and VI.
On Translating Homer.   Part III.

THEOLOGICAL.

Hellenism and Hebraism.   Culture and Anarchy.   Chap. IV.
St. Paul's Ideas of Righteousness.   St. Paul and Puritanism.
  Chap. I.
The Church of England.
Religion New Given.   Chapter III.
Literature and Dogma.
The Testimony of Jesus to Himself.   Literature and Dogma.
  Chapter VII.   Parts III., IV., and V.

SOCIAL.

Sweetness and Light.   Culture and Anarchy.   Chapter I.
Barbarians, Philistines, Populace.   Culture and Anarchy.
  Chapter III.

## POLITICAL.

My Countrymen. Friendship's Garland.
Democracy. Mixed Essays.
The Failure of Liberalism. Irish Essays.
Civilization in the United States. Nineteenth Century.
April, 1888.

## EDUCATIONAL.

Porro unum est necessarium. Mixed Essays.
Armenius on Compulsory Education. Friendship's Garland.
Letters 6 and 7.
A Speech at Eton. Irish Essays.
Literature and Science — A Lecture.

## LITERARY.

Preface to First Edition of Poems. 1853.
A Guide to English Literature. Mixed Essays.
The Function of Criticism at the Present Time. Essays in
Criticism.
George Sand. Mixed Essays.
Maurice de Guèrin. Essays in Criticism.
Joubert. Essays in Criticism.
A French Critic on Voltaire. Miscellaneous Essays.
Emerson. (A Lecture.)

### Selected Books of Reference on Matthew Arnold and his Works.

Poems by Matthew Arnold. Frazer's Magazine. February,
1854.
Review of Matthew Arnold's Poems of 1853. North British
Review. February–August, 1854.
New English Poets. Putnam's Magazine. September, 1855.

Matthew Arnold's Merope.  Frazer's Magazine.  June, 1858.

The Critical Character.  Westminster Review.  October, 1863.

Essays in Criticism.  North British Review.  March–June, 1865.

Matthew Arnold, Poet and Essayist.  British Quarterly. Review.  October, 1865.

Arnold on the Study of Celtic Literature.  By Robert Giffen.  Fortnightly Review.  July, 1867.

The Prophet of Culture.  By Henry Sidgwick.  Macmillan's Magazine.  August, 1867.

Mr. Arnold's New Poems.  By A. C. Swinburne.  Fortnightly Review.  September, 1867.

Mr. Arnold and Mr. Swinburne.  By Peter Bayne.  Contemporary Review.  September–December, 1867.

William Morris and Matthew Arnold.  By Shirley (J. Skelton).  Frazer's Magazine.  February, 1869.

Mr. Arnold and Anarchy.  New Englander.  January, 1870.

Matthew Arnold and Puritanism.  British Quarterly Review. October, 1870.

Matthew Arnold and the Church of England.  By Leslie Stephen.  Frazer's Magazine.  October, 1870.

Amateur Theology.  Literature and Dogma.  Blackwood's Magazine.  June, 1873.

Literature and Dogma.  By F. H. Newman.  Frazer's Magazine.  July, 1873.

A Representative Triad ; Hood, Arnold, Procter.  By E. C. Stedman.  Scribner's Magazine.  February, 1874.

Matthew Arnold's Literature and Dogma.  By J. M. Sturtevant.  New Englander.  January, 1875.

Victorian Poets.  (Matthew Arnold.)  By E. C. Stedman. 1876.

Essays in Literary Criticism (The Poetry of Matthew Arnold). By R. H. Hutton. 1876.

Mr. Arnold on Butler. British Quarterly Review. July, 1877.

Some Aspects of Matthew Arnold's Poetry. By G. S. Merriam. Scribner's Magazine. June, 1879.

Matthew Arnold. By Andrew Lang. The Century. April, 1882.

Matthew Arnold. By Hamilton W. Mabie. The Christian Union. October 28, 1883.

Arnold on Emerson and Carlyle. By John Burroughs. The Century. April, 1884.

Matthew Arnold as a Poet. By Harriet Waters Preston. Atlantic Monthly. May, 1884.

Matthew Arnold. By E. P. Whipple. North American Review. May, 1884.

Newman and Arnold. By R. H. Hutton. Contemporary Review. March, 1886.

Prose Remains (Review of Poems by Matthew Arnold). By A. H. Clough. 1888.

Matthew Arnold Memorial Number. Pall Mall Gazette. April 19, 1888.

Matthew Arnold on America. By Joel Benton. The Christian Union. April 28, 1888.

Arnold's Place in Literature. By Edward J. Harding. The Critic. April 28, 1888.

Criticism of Matthew Arnold. By John Burroughs. The Century. June, 1888.

The Poetry of Matthew Arnold. By Vida D. Scudder. Andover Review. September, 1888.

Matthew Arnold. Quarterly Review. October, 1888.

Matthew Arnold. By Augustine Birrell. Scribner's Magazine. November, 1888.

# AMERICAN AUTHORS.

# A Guide to the Study of Nineteenth Century Authors.

## By LOUISE MANNING HODGKINS,

PROFESSOR OF ENGLISH LITERATURE IN WELLESLEY COLLEGE.

Copyright, 1888.

---

## WASHINGTON IRVING, 1783-1859.

### Pseudonyms of Irving.

Simeon Senex (?).
Jonathan Oldstyle.
Launcelot Langstaff.
Diedrich Knickerbocker.
Fray Antonio Agapida.
Geoffrey Crayon.

NOTE. — Irving is called

The Dutch Herodotus.
The Father of American Letters.
The Addison of American Literature.
The First Ambassador sent by the New
World of Letters to the Old.

### Significant Facts in the Life of Washington Irving

The Name and Blessing of Washington.
Desultory Education.
Early European Travels. 1804-1806.

Death of Miss Hoffman.   1809.
Publication of Knickerbocker.   1809.
Residence in Europe.   1815-1832.
Friendship of Walter Scott.   1817-1859.
Financial Reverses of 1818.
Publication of the Sketch Book.   1819-1820.
Secretary of Legation at Court of St. James.   1829-1831.
Gold Medal of the Royal Society of Literature.   1830.
D. C. L. of Oxford.   1831.
Reception in New York.   1832.
Life in Spain.   (Minister to Spain.)   1842-1846.
Retired Life at Sunnyside, Tarrytown, N.Y.   1846-1859.

### Biographical Writings.

*Chief Biographer of Irving.   Pierre Irving.   1862.*
Legend of Sleepy Hollow.   By Washington Irving.   1820.
Gallery of Literary Characters.   (Portrait in Youth.)   Fraser's
    Magazine.   November, 1831.
A Fable for the Critics.   By James Russell Lowell.   1848.
Wolfert's Roost.   By Washington Irving.   1855.
Sunnyside.   (Fine illustrations of Irving's Home.)   Harper's
    Magazine.   December, 1856.
Recollections of Irving.   By George P. Putnam.   Atlantic
    Monthly.   November, 1860.
Dream Life.   (Preface.)   By Ik. Marvel.   (Donald G.
    Mitchell.)   1863.
The Home of Washington Irving.   (Illustrated folio.)   By
    Rev. Edmund Guilbert.   1867.
Washington Irving.   By David J. Hill.   (American Authors
    Series.)   1879.
Washington Irving.   By Charles Dudley Warner.   (American
    Men of Letters Series.)   1881.

For copy of Gilbert Stuart Newton's portrait of Irving, now in possession of John Murray, Esq., of London, see Harper's Magazine. April, 1883.
Washington Irving. A Commemoration of the One Hundredth Anniversary of his Birth. By the Washington Irving Association. 1884.
A Glimpse of Washington Irving at Home. By Clarence Cook. Century Magazine. May, 1887.

### Poems on Washington Irving.

In the Churchyard at Tarrytown. A Sonnet. By H. W. Longfellow.
A Fable for the Critics. (Irving.) By James Russell Lowell.
Washington Irving. A Centennial Poem. By R. H. Thayer.
See Irving Centenary Number of the Critic in Books of Reference.

### A Group of Irving's Friends.

James K. Paulding.
Henry Brevoort.
Washington Allston.
Sir Walter Scott.
Thomas Moore.
Samuel Rogers.
. Talma.
George P. Putnam.

Charles Robert Leslie.
W. M. Thackeray.
George Bancroft.
W. H. Prescott.
Prince Dolgorouki.
James Fenimore Cooper.
Nathaniel P. Willis.

### Ten Selected Works.

| | |
|---|---|
| Knickerbocker, | 1809. |
| Sketch Book, | 1819–1820. |
| Bracebridge Hall, | 1822. |
| Tales of a Traveller, | 1824. |
| Columbus, | 1828. |

| Conquest of Granada, | 1829. |
| Alhambra, | 1832. |
| Crayon Miscellany, | 1835. |
| Wolfert's Roost, | 1855. |
| Life of Washington, | 1855–1859. |

Number of works written by Washington Irving, 17.
Date of publication, 1807–1859.

**Selections from the Works of Irving.**

Knickerbocker's History of New York.
  Wouter Van Twiller.   Book III, chap. 1.
  The Manners of our Grandfathers.   Book III, chap. 3.
  Peter the Headstrong.   Book I, chap. 1.

Sketch Book.

| Rip Van Winkle. | Christmas Papers. |
| Rural Funerals. | Legend of Sleepy Hollow. |
| Westminster Abbey. | |

Bracebridge Hall.

| Ready-Money Jack. | May Day Customs. |
| The Stout Gentleman. | The Schoolmaster |
| A Literary Antiquary. | The Rookery. |
| St. Mark's Eve. | The Wedding. |

Tales of a Traveller.

| Buckthorn. | Wolfert Webber. |

Columbus.

  First Landing of Columbus in the New World.   Vol. I,
    Book IV.

Conquest of Granada.

  How Queen Isabella arrived at the Camp.   Chap. 80.
  Surrender of Granada.   Chap. 99.

Alhambra.

> Palace of the Alhambra.
> The Mysterious Chambers.      •
> Legend of Prince Ahmed Al Kamel.
> Court of Lions.

Crayon Miscellany.

> Abbotsford.                    Newstead Abbey.

Mahomet and his Successors.  The Alexandrian Library.  Vol.
II, chap. 24.

Wolfert's Roost.

> Wolfert's Roost.               Broek : the Dutch Paradise.

Life of Washington.

> The American Army.  Vol. I, chap. 12.
> Washington in Command.  Vol. II, chap. 1.
> Washington at Valley Forge.  Vol. III, chap. 31.
> Siege and Surrender of Yorktown.  Vol. IV, chap. 28.
> Washington's Farewell Address.  Vol. V, chap. 30.

**Selected Books of Reference on Washington Irving and
his Works.**

The Sketch Book.  (A good defence of American Literature.)  By R. H. Dana.  North American Review.
September, 1819.

On the Writings of Charles Brockden Brown and Washington Irving.  (An answer to the American protest on the
character of American Literature.)  By John Wilson.
Blackwood's Magazine.  February, 1820.

The Sketch Book.  (An illustration of the early patronizing
review.)  By F. Jeffrey.  Edinburgh Review.  August, 1820.

Bracebridge Hall.  By F. Jeffrey.  Edinburgh Review.
November, 1822.

A Chronicle of the Conquest of Granada. By W. H. Prescott. North American Review. October, 1829.

A Tour on the Prairies. By Edward Everett. North American Review. July, 1830.

Alhambra. By A. H. Everett. North American Review. October, 1832.

American Authorship. (Washington Irving.) Littell's Living Age. (From the New Monthly Magazine.) June 11, 1853.

Life of George Washington. (For comparison of Irving's style with Bancroft's and Prescott's.) By G. W. Greene. North American Review. April, 1858.

Eulogy on Washington Irving. By Wm. C. Bryant. 1860. (In Life of W. C. Bryant by Parke Godwin. Vol. II, chap. 32.)

Nil Nisi Bonum. By William M. Thackeray. Harper's Magazine. March, 1860.

Washington Irving. By James Wynne. Harper's Magazine. February, 1862.

Washington Irving. By Donald G. Mitchell. Atlantic Monthly. June, 1864.

Poe, Irving, Hawthorne. By G. P. Lathrop. Scribner's Monthly. April, 1876.

Bibliography of Irving. The Critic. (Irving Centenary Number.) March 31, 1883.

Hap-hazard Personalities. (Irving.) By Charles Lanman. Literary World. April 21, 1883.

American Humorists. By H. R. Haweis. 1883.

Bryant and his Friends. (Washington Irving.) By James Grant Wilson. 1886.

American Literature. By Edwin Percy Whipple. 1887.

American Literature. 1607–1885. (Washington Irving.) By Charles F. Richardson. 1887.

# A Guide to the Study of Nineteenth Century Authors.

By LOUISE MANNING HODGKINS,

PROFESSOR OF ENGLISH LITERATURE IN WELLESLEY COLLEGE.

Copyright, 1888.

---

## WILLIAM CULLEN BRYANT, 1794-1878.

### Names Given to Bryant.

The American Wordsworth.
The Founder of American Poetry.
The First Representative Poet of America.
The First Poet of American Nature.

### Significant Facts in the Life of William Cullen Bryant.

Poetic precocity.
Degree of Williams College (with less than one year in residence, 1810–1811), 1819.
Publication of Thanatopsis, 1817.
Legal life, 1815–1825.
Marriage to Miss Frances Fairchild, 1821.
Removal to New York City, 1825.
Literary friendships.
Foreign travel.
Journalistic life, 1828–1878.
Attitude on the slavery question, and advocacy of equal rights.

Admission to the Russian Academy, 1873.
Seventieth and Eightieth Birthday Celebrations, 1864 and 1874.

**Biographical Writings.**

*Chief Biographer,* PARKE GODWIN, 1883.

**Other Contributions to Bryant's Biography.**

The Life and Letters of Catharine Sedgwick. (A pen portrait of Bryant in 1822.) Letter from Miss Sedgwick to her brother Charles. February 2, 1822.
Homes of American Authors. (W. C. Bryant.) By George W. Curtis. 1853.
The Bryant Vase. By Dr. Samuel Osgood. Harper's Magazine. July, 1876.
The Boys of My Boyhood. By W. C. Bryant. St. Nicholas. December, 1876.
William Cullen Bryant. By Horatio N. Powers. Scribner's Magazine. August, 1878. (For Wyatt Eaton's portrait of 1878. Excellently illustrated.)
William Cullen Bryant. American Authors Series. By David J. Hill. 1879.
William Cullen Bryant. By A. J. Symington. 1880.
Poets of America. (Bryant.) By E. C. Stedman. 1885.
Bryant and His Friends. By James Grant Wilson. 1886.

**Poems Contributory to his own Biography.**

Entrance to a Wood.
To a Waterfowl.
Green River.
Oh, Fairest of the Rural Maids.
Hymn to Death.

Death of the Flowers.
The Future Life.
The Life that Is.
October, 1866.   (On the death of Mrs. Bryant.)
A Lifetime.

### Poems on Bryant.

Panegyrists of Bryant's Seventieth Birthday.

| | |
|---|---|
| Bayard Taylor. | J. G. Whittier. |
| O. W. Holmes. | A. B. Street. |
| G. H. Boker. | Mary C. Booth. |
| R. H. Stoddard. | J. R. Lowell. |
| Julia Ward Howe. | H. T. Tuckerman. |

Poets of Bryant's death.

| | |
|---|---|
| E. C. Stedman. | R. H. Stoddard. |
| Bayard Taylor. | O. W. Holmes. |

### Orations on Bryant.

G. W. Curtis, New York Historical Society.
R. C. Waterston, before the Mass. Historical Society.
Dr. Samuel Osgood, at Goethe Club.
John Bigelow, before the Century Club.

The poet whom Bryant most loved, — Wordsworth.
A poet with whom he found much fault, — Browning.
A poetess whom he esteemed, — Mrs. Browning.
Poets with whom he had no sympathy, — Byron, Rossetti
A poet whom he admired, — William Morris.
A poet whom he detested, — Swinburne.

**A Group of Bryant's American Literary Friends.**

| *Early.* | *Later.* |
|---|---|
| W. E. Channing. | H. W. Longfellow. |
| J. Audubon. | N. Hawthorne. |
| W. Allston. | R. W. Emerson. |
| F. G. Halleck. | O. W. Holmes. |
| J. R. Drake. | J. G. Whittier. |
| J. F. Cooper. | J. R. Lowell. |
| J. A. Hillhouse. | G. W. Curtis. |
| J. G. Percival. | R. H. Stoddard. |
| J. Pierpont. | E. C. Stedman. |
| W. Irving. | P. Godwin. |
| J. K. Paulding. | J. C. Wilson. |
| R. C. Sands. | E. Everett. |
| W. H. Prescott. | R. C. Waterston. |
| C. Sedgwick. | Dr. S. Osgood. |
| George Bancroft. | |

**A Life-Long Friend.**

Richard Henry Dana.

**A Group of Bryant's Art Friends.**

| | |
|---|---|
| S. F. B. Morse. | A. B. Durand. |
| R. W. Weir. | Henry Inman. |
| Daniel Huntington. | Thomas Cole. |
| C. C. Ingham. | |

Note. — Bryant is introduced in Durand's view of the Catskills.

**Selections from Bryant's Poems.**

Poems of Patriotism.

| | |
|---|---|
| Seventy-Six. | Our Country's Call. |
| The Antiquity of Freedom. | The Twenty-Second of |
| Oh, Mother of a Mighty Race. | February. |

Poems of Nature.

| | |
|---|---|
| The Yellow Violet. | The Evening Wind. |
| Summer Wind. | To the Fringed Gentian. |
| After a Tempest. | The Fountain. |
| Autumn Woods. | The Planting of the Apple |
| To a Cloud. | Tree. |
| The Forest Hymn. | The Snow Shower. |
| June. | Robert of Lincoln. |
| The Gladness of Nature. | The Song of the Sower. |
| Sonnet on October. | Return of the Birds. |

NOTE. — "Of one hundred and seventy-one poems by Bryant, more than a hundred treat of some natural object, scene, or phenomenon " — D. J. HILL.

Poems of Life and Death.

| | |
|---|---|
| Thanatopsis. | The Future Life. |
| The Two Graves. | The Return of Youth. |
| Innocent Child and Snow- | The Crowded Street. |
| White Flower. | The Land of Dreams. |
| Life. | The Two Travellers. |
| The Battle-Field. | The Flood of Years. |

On Human Slavery.

The African Chief.
The Death of Slavery.

Humorous.

To a Mosquito.
Rhode Island Coal.

Personal Poems.

Dante.
Abraham Lincoln.
John Lothrop Motley.

Hellenic Verses.

> The Massacre at Scio.
> The Song of the Greek Amazon.
> The Greek Partisan.
> The Greek Boy.

Hymns.

> " Deem not that they are blest alone."
> " Thou whose unmeasured temple stands."
> The Centennial Hymn.

Translations.

> Spring-time.   (From the Spanish.)
> Love and Folly.   (From the French.)
> It is a Fearful Night.   (From the Portuguese.)
> There sits a Lovely Maiden.   (From the German )
> The Order of Nature.   (From the Latin.)
> The Swallow.   (From the Italian.)
> The Iliad and Odyssey.

### A Group of Translators of the Iliad and Odyssey.

| | |
|---|---|
| George Chapman. | Ichabod Charles Wright. |
| Alexander Pope. | Francis W. Newman.   (The Iliad.) |
| William Cowper. | William C. Bryant. |
| William Sotheby. | William Morris.   (The Odyssey.) |

### Specimens of Bryant's Prose.

On American Poetry.   North American Review.   July, 1818.

Letters from the East.   Contributed to the Evening Post 1853–1854.

**Works Edited by Bryant.**

The Talisman, 1829–1830.
History of the United States.
The Library of Poetry and Song.

**Specimens of Bryant's Prose Orations.**

Cooper.                Scott.
Irving.                Mazzini.
Morse.

**Selected Books of Reference on William Cullen Bryant
and his Works.**

American Writers. (A severe criticism on American Litera-
ture in general and Bryant's Poetry in particular.) Black-
wood's Magazine. September, 1824.
Bryant's Poems. (Specimen of an early favorable review.)
Foreign Quarterly Review. August and October, 1832.
Bryant's Poems. (The Fountain and Others.) North
American Review. October, 1842.
Literati. (William Cullen Bryant.) By Edgar A. Poe. 1850.
American Authorship. (William Cullen Bryant.) Littell's
Living Age. December 10, 1853.
Essays: Critical and Imaginative. (American Poetry:
Bryant.) By John Wilson. 1857.
Bryant. By G. S. Hillard. Atlantic Monthly. February,
1864.
Literature and Life. (Bryant.) By E. P. Whipple. 1871.
Critical Essays and Literary Notes. By Bayard Taylor. 1876.
Address before the New York Historical Society. By Geo.
W. Curtis. 1878.
William Cullen Bryant. By E. S. Nadal. Macmillan's
Magazine. May–October, 1878.

Memorial Address before the **Century** Club.   By John Bigelow.   November 12, 1878.

Address before the **Massachusetts** Historical Society.   By Robert C. Winthrop.   1879.

Afternoons with the Poets.   (A discussion of Bryant's Sonnets.)   By Charles D. Deshler.   1879.

The National Academy of the Arts of Design.   By B. J Lossing.   Harper's Magazine.   May, 1883.

# A Guide to the Study of Nineteenth Century Authors.

By LOUISE MANNING HODGKINS,

PROFESSOR OF ENGLISH LITERATURE IN WELLESLEY COLLEGE.

Copyright, 1888.

---

## NATHANIEL HAWTHORNE, 1804-1864.

### Significant Facts in the Life of Hawthorne.

Early Life in Salem, Massachusetts.
Tutelage under Joseph Worcester (Author of the Dictionary). 1811–1818.
Education at Bowdoin College. 1821–1825.
Failure of Early Publications.
Life in Lenox and Concord. 1842–1851, 1860–1864.
Custom-House Life. 1846–1849.
Publication of the Scarlet Letter. 1850.
Consulship at Liverpool. 1853–1857.
Life in Italy. 1858.
Attitude during the Civil War.

### Biographical Writings.

Hawthorne. By Oliver Wendell Holmes. Atlantic Monthly. July, 1864.
Nathaniel Hawthorne. (Illustrated.) By R. H. Stoddard. Harper's Magazine. October, 1872.

15

Yesterdays with Authors.  (Hawthorne.)  By James T. Fields. 1876.

A Study of Hawthorne.  By George P. Lathrop.  1876.

Home Life of the Brook Farm Association.  Atlantic Monthly.  October and November, 1878.

Hawthorne.  By Henry James.  English Men of Letters Series.  1880.

Hawthorne and his Friends.  By George H. Holden. Harper's Magazine.  July, 1881.

Nathaniel Hawthorne and his Wife.  By Julian Hawthorne. 1885.

**Sketches from Hawthorne which contribute to his own Biography.**

The Gentle Boy.
The Seven Vagabonds.
Little Annie's Ramble.
Preface to Snow Image.
The Devil in Manuscript.
Prologue to the Scarlet Letter.

**A Group of Hawthorne's Friends.**

Horatio Bridge.
Franklin Pierce.
William B. Pike.
Ellery Channing.
A. Bronson Alcott.
Henry Thoreau.
Ralph Waldo Emerson.
James T. Fields.
Charles Sumner.

Edwin P. Whipple.
James Hillard.
Henry W. Longfellow.
Colonel Hibbard.
George Ticknor.
Hermann Melville.
J. L. Motley.
Oliver W. Holmes.
James Freeman Clarke.

Selections from Hawthorne's Tales and Sketches

ILLUSTRATIVE OF EARLY NEW ENGLAND HISTORY.

The Grey Champion.
The Maypole of Merrymount.
Legends of the Province House.
Old News.
Old Ticonderoga.
My Kinsman — Mayor Molineux.
Endicott and the Red Cross.

NATURE STUDIES.

The Snow Flakes.
Footprints on the Seashore.
Birds and Bird Voices.
Night Sketches.

ALLEGORICAL TALES.

A Rill from the Town Pump.
The Great Carbuncle.
The Sister Years.
The Snow Image.
The Great Stone Face.
Rappaccini's Daughter.
The Artist of the Beautiful.

MISCELLANEOUS.

Wakefield.
The Minister's Black Veil.
Chippings with a Chisel.
Young Goodman Brown.
Roger Malvin's Burial.

### Four Most Celebrated Romances.

Scarlet Letter.
The House of Seven Gables.
The Blithedale Romance.
The Marble Faun.

Number of Romances by Hawthorne, finished and unfinished, nine.

NOTE. — The Marble Faun was published in London under the title of Transformation.

### Classics for Children.

The Wonder Book.          Tanglewood Tales

### Works which were the Result of Hawthorne's Travels.

Our Old Home.
French, Italian, and American Note Books.
The Marble Faun.

### Selected Books of Reference on Nathaniel Hawthorne and his Works.

Twice Told Tales.  By H. W. Longfellow.  North American Review.  July, 1837.

Nathaniel Hawthorne.  By S. W. S. Dutton.  New Englander.  January, 1847.

A Fable for the Critics.  (Hawthorne.)  By James Russell Lowell.  1848.

Literati.  (Hawthorne.)  By Edgar Allen Poe.  1850.

Scarlet Letter.  By A. W. Abbott.  North American Review.  July, 1850.

Recollections of a Literary Life.  (American Prose Writer.)  By M. R. Mitford.  1852.

Mental Portraits.  (Hawthorne.)  By H. T. Tuckerman.  1853

House of Seven Gables and Blithedale Romance. By A.
P. Peabody. North American Review. January, 1853.
American Authorship. No. III. (Nathaniel Hawthorne.)
Littell's Living Age. July 16, 1853.
Illustrations of Genius. (The Scarlet Letter.) By Henry
Giles. 1854.
Brief Biographies. (Hawthorne.) By Samuel Smiles. 1860.
Nathaniel Hawthorne. By E. P. Whipple. Atlantic
Monthly. May, 1860.
Mr. Hawthorne's Transformation. North British Review.
August–November, 1860.
The Blithedale Romance. (From the New Monthly Maga-
zine.) Littell's Living Age. August, 1862.
Hawthorne on England. Blackwood's Magazine. Novem-
ber, 1863.
Dreamthorp. (A Shelf in my Bookcase.) By Alexander
Smith. 1864.
New Englanders and the Old Home. Quarterly Review.
January, 1864.
Nathaniel Hawthorne. By George William Curtis. North
American Review. October, 1864.
Genius of Hawthorne; a Review of the Marble Faun. By
E. P. Peabody. Atlantic Monthly. September, 1868.
Nathaniel Hawthorne. North British Review. September–
December, 1868.
Review of the American Note Books. Littell's Living Age.
(From the London Saturday Review and Spectator.)
January–March, 1869.
The English Note Books of Nathaniel Hawthorne. By
G. S. Hillard. Atlantic Monthly. September, 1870.
Nathaniel Hawthorne. Littell's Living Age. June 17, 1871.
Scenes from the Marble Faun. By W. S. Alden. Scribner's
Magazine. September, 1871.

Concord Days. (Hawthorne.) By A. Bronson Alcott. 1872.

History of Hawthorne's Last Romance. (Septimius Felton.) By G. P. Lathrop. Atlantic Monthly. October, 1872.

Hawthorne's Last Bequest. By T. W. Higginson. Scribner's Magazine. November, 1872.

Hours in a Library. (Hawthorne.) By Leslie Stephen. 1875.

Poets and Novelists. (Hawthorne.) By George Barnet Smith. 1876.

Essays in Literary Criticisms. (Hawthorne.) By R. H. Hutton. 1876.

Nathaniel Hawthorne. By R. H. Stoddard. Encyclopedia Britannica. 1879.

The Genius of Nathaniel Hawthorne. By Anthony Trollope. North American Review. September, 1879.

Hawthorne. By Julia Ward Howe. The Critic. 1881.

The Hawthorne Index. 1882.

Literary Life. (Hawthorne.) By W. Shepherd. 1882.

Three Americans and Three Englishmen. (Hawthorne.) By C. F. Johnson. 1886.

Hawthorne's Philosophy. By Julian Hawthorne. Century Magazine. May, 1886.

# A Guide to the Study of Nineteenth Century Authors.

## By LOUISE MANNING HODGKINS,

PROFESSOR OF ENGLISH LITERATURE IN WELLESLEY COLLEGE.

Copyright, 1888.

---

## RALPH WALDO EMERSON, 1803-1882.

### Significant Facts in the Life of R. W. Emerson.

Ancestry.  (Through eight generations of clergymen.)

Education. { Boston Latin School.
{ Harvard College (Degree, 1821).

Boston School Teacher.  1822–1825.

Student of Divinity.  1823–1827.

Ordination as Colleague of Henry Ware.  1829.

Second Marriage.  1835.

Visits to Europe.  1832 and 1847.

First Course of Lectures in Boston.  1836.

Publication of First Volume of Essays.  1841.

Publication of First Volume of Poems.  1847.

Degree of LL.D. at Harvard.  1866.

### Biographical Writings.

*Chief Biographer of Emerson*, JAMES ELLIOT CABOT, *1887*

Twice Told Tales. (The Great Stone Face.)  By Nathaniel Hawthorne.  1851.  (Ernest in this story is said to be Emerson.)

Homes of the New World. By Frederika Bremer. 1853.
Homes and Haunts of Emerson. By M. P. Sanborn.
Scribner's Monthly. February, 1879.
The Concord Guide-Book. (Emerson's Home.) By G.
B. Bartlett. 1880.
The Literary World. Emerson Number. May 22, 1880.
Ralph Waldo Emerson : his Life, Writings, and Philosophy.
By George Willis Cooke. 1881.
In Memoriam : Ralph Waldo Emerson. By Alexander Ire-
land. 1882.
Some Recollections of Ralph Waldo Emerson. By E. P.
Whipple. Harper's Magazine. September, 1882.
Correspondence of Thomas Carlyle and Ralph Waldo Emer-
son. 1883.
Ralph Waldo Emerson. By Oliver Wendell Holmes. 1885.
Ralph Waldo Emerson. His Maternal Ancestors. By D.
G. Haskins. 1886.

**Poems of Emerson contributing to his own Biography.**

Good-bye.[1]                    Dirge.
To Ellen.                       Threnody.
" I grieve that better souls than mine."
Walden.                         Terminus.

Emerson's favorite philosopher  . .  Plato.
  "           "      historian . . . .  Plutarch.
  "           "      essayist . . . .  Montaigne.
  "           "      poet. . . . . .  Shakespeare.

NOTE. — Emerson mentions Shakespeare 112 times.

---

[1] This poem, popularly supposed to date from Emerson's retirement
from the ministry, was written when he was a Boston school teacher.

## A Group of Social, Political, and Religious Reformers.
### 1820-1845.

| | |
|---|---|
| R. W. Emerson. | Theodore Parker. |
| A. B. Alcott. | Geo. Wm. Curtis. |
| N. Hawthorne. | Wm. H. Channing. |
| Margaret Fuller. | James F. Clarke. |
| Henry Thoreau. | F. H. Hedge. |
| George Ripley. | Edward Everett. |
| E. P. Peabody. | Wm. E. Channing. |

### Selections from Emerson's Essays.

| | |
|---|---|
| Landor. | Carlyle. |
| Coleridge. | |

| | |
|---|---|
| Self Reliance. | Behavior. |
| Friendship. | Beauty. |
| Character. | Courage. |
| Manners. | Success. |
| Nature. | Social Aims. |
| Wealth. | Inspiration. |
| Culture. | Greatness. |

| | |
|---|---|
| Plato. | Goethe. |
| Montaigne. | Shakespeare. |

NOTE. — Emerson is most indebted to Plato and Montaigne

### Selections from Emerson's Orations.

The American Scholar.
Literary Ethics.
New England Reformers.

### Selections from Emerson's Poems.

#### POEMS OF NATURE.

| | |
|---|---|
| The Rhodora. | Monadnoc. |
| The Humble Bee. | The Titmouse. |
| The Snow-Storm. | Song of Nature. |
| Wood-notes. | |

#### PATRIOTIC.

| | |
|---|---|
| Concord Hymn. | Voluntaries. No. III. |
| Boston Hymn. | Freedom. |

#### Religious Hymns.

"We love the venerable house our fathers built to God."

#### A Collection of Poems edited by Emerson.

Parnassus. 1874.

#### Miscellaneous Poems.

| | |
|---|---|
| The Sphinx. | Sursum Corda. |
| The Problem. | The Apology. |
| The World's Soul. | Brahma. |
| Compensation. | The Test. |

#### A Group of Makers of the North American Review.

| | |
|---|---|
| Daniel Webster. | 1782–1852. |
| R. H. Dana. | 1787–1879. |
| Jared Sparks. | 1789–1866. |
| Edward Everett. | 1794–1865. |
| Wm. H. Prescott. | 1796–1850. |
| John G. Palfrey. | 1796–1881. |
| George Bancroft. | 1800–    . |

R. W. Emerson.        1803–1882.
H. W. Longfellow.     1807–1882.
G. S. Hillard.        1808–1879.
Charles Sumner.       1811–1874.
A. P. Peabody.        1811–    .
John L. Motley.       1814–1877.
J. R. Lowell.         1819–    .
C. E. Norton.         1827–    .

### Selected Books of Reference on Ralph Waldo Emerson and his Works.

Emerson. Blackwood's Magazine. December, 1847.

The Connection between Science, Literature, and Religion. By George Gilfillan. 1848.

Emerson's Representative Men. By Charles Eliot Norton. North American Review. April, 1850.

Emerson's English Traits. Westminster Review. October, 1856.                                  –

Recent Lectures and Writings of Emerson. Frazer's Magazine. May, 1867.

Mr. Emerson's Poems. By Charles Eliot Norton. The Nation. May 30, 1867.

Ralph Waldo Emerson. North British Review. September–December, 1867.

The Culture of Emerson. By M. D. Conway. Frazer's Magazine. July, 1868.

Emerson's Society and Solitude. By I. N. Tarbox. Frazer's Magazine. July, 1870.

My Study Windows. (Emerson, the Lecturer.) By James Russell Lowell. 1871.

Mr. Emerson's Philosophy. By H. W. Holland. The Nation. November 17, 1871.

Short Studies. By J. A. Froude. 1873.

The First Century of the Republic. By E. P. Whipple. Harper's Magazine. February, 1876.

Recollections of Writers. (Emerson.) By Charles and Mary Cowden Clarke. 1878.

Birds and Poets. (A Word or Two on Emerson.) By John Burroughs. 1879.

The Homes and Haunts of Emerson. By F. B. Sanborn. Scribner's Monthly. February, 1879.

Emerson's Theism. New York Independent. March 13, 1880.

Ralph Waldo Emerson. By F. H. Underwood. North American Review. May, 1880.

Ralph Waldo Emerson, Philosopher and Poet. By A. H. Guernsey. 1881.

Discourses on America. (Emerson.) By Matthew Arnold. 1882.

Emerson at Home and Abroad. By M. D. Conway. 1882.

Emerson as a Poet. By E. P. Whipple. North American Review. July, 1882.

The Transcendentalism of New England. By John Orr. The International Review. October, 1882.

Emerson and Carlyle. By E. P. Whipple. North American Review. May, 1883.

Emerson as a Poet. By Joel Benton. 1883.

Poets of America. (Emerson.) By E. C. Stedman. 1885.

Literary Remains. (Mr. Emerson.) By H. James. 1885.

The Genius and Character of Ralph Waldo Emerson. By F. B. Sanborn. 1885.

Holmes' Life of Emerson. By George Bancroft. North American Review. February, 1885.

Ralph Waldo Emerson. By W. L. Courtney. Fortnightly Review. September, 1885.

Recollections of Eminent Men. (Emerson.) By E. P. Whipple. 1886.

The Optimism of Ralph Waldo Emerson. By W. F. Dana. 1886.

Critical Miscellanies. (Emerson.) By J. Morley. 1886.

The Influence of Emerson. By W. F. Thayer. 1886.

Men and Letters. (Emerson's Self.) By H. E. Scudder. 1887.

Obiter Dicta. Series II. (Emerson.) By Augustine Birrell. 1887.

Emerson. By Gamaliel Bradford, Jr. New Princeton Review. March, 1888.

# A Guide to the Study of Nineteenth Century Authors.

By LOUISE MANNING HODGKINS,

PROFESSOR OF ENGLISH LITERATURE IN WELLESLEY COLLEGE.

Copyright, 1888.

—.  —

## HENRY WADSWORTH LONGFELLOW,
## 1807-1882.

### Significant Facts in the Life of Longfellow.

Maternal Descent from John Alden.

Boyhood in Portland, Me.  1807-1821.

Education at Bowdoin College.  1821-1825.

Election to Professorship of Modern Languages at Bowdoin.  1825.

First Residence Abroad.  1826-1829.

Professor of Modern Languages at Bowdoin College.  1829-1835.

Publication of First Book.  1833.

Successor of Professor Ticknor, at Harvard College.  1835.

Second Residence Abroad.  1835-1836.

Professor at Harvard College.  1836-1854.

One of the Original Contributors to the Atlantic Monthly, founded 1857.

Retired Citizen and Poet.  1854-1882.

### Biographical Writings.

*Chief Biographer of Longfellow*, SAMUEL LONGFELLOW. 1886.

Henry Wadsworth Longfellow. (Illustrated.) By R. H. Stoddard. Scribner's Magazine. September, 1878.

Henry Wadsworth Longfellow. A Biographical Sketch. By Francis H. Underwood. 1882.

Henry Wadsworth Longfellow. By W. S. Kennedy. 1882.

Death of Longfellow. By Walt Whitman. Critic. April 8, 1882.

Glimpses of Longfellow in Social Life. By Annie Fields. Century Magazine. April, 1886.

Henry W. Longfellow. By George Lowell. 1887.

Longfellow. By Professor Eric S. Robertson. Great Writers Series. 1887.

Final Memorials of Longfellow. Edited by Samuel Longfellow. 1888.

### Poems of Longfellow contributing to his Own Biography.

The Courtship of Miles Standish.
The Psalm of Life.
Footsteps of Angels.
In the Long Sleepless Watches of the Night.
The Old Clock on the Stairs.
To the River Charles.
A Gleam of Sunshine.
The Two Angels.
My Lost Youth.
The Children's Hour.
Three Friends of Mine.
Morituri Salutamus.
From my Arm-Chair.

### A Group of Poems on Longfellow.

To Longfellow.   By Denis F. MacCarthy.
Longfellow's Birthday.   By James Russell Lowell.
To Henry Wadsworth Longfellow.   By O. W. Holmes.
Henry Wadsworth Longfellow.   By Helen Gray Cone.
Vale et Salve.   By Edith M. Thomas.

See also Longfellow Number of the Literary World, February 26, 1881

### A Group of Contemporary Poets.

| American. | English. |
|---|---|
| Dana. | Wordsworth. |
| Drake. | Coleridge. |
| Halleck. | Moore. |
| Poe. | Campbell. |
| Bryant. | Hood. |
| Emerson. | Keble. |
| Holmes. | Clough. |
| Whittier. | The Brownings. |
| Lowell. | Tennyson. |

### The Saturday Club,

that projected THE ATLANTIC MONTHLY at a dinner in 1856.

| | |
|---|---|
| Louis Agassiz. | Judge E. R. Hoar. |
| J. Eliot Cabot. | Dr. Estes Howe. |
| John S. Dwight. | Henry W. Longfellow. |
| Ralph W. Emerson. | James R. Lowell. |
| C. C. Felton. | Charles E. Morton. |
| Oliver W. Holmes. | Edmund Quincy. |

NOTE. — Dr. Holmes gave the magazine its name, and J. R. Lowell was its first editor.

**Languages into which Longfellow has been translated.**

| | |
|---|---|
| French. | Italian. |
| German. | Portuguese. |
| Dutch. | Spanish. |
| Swedish. | Polish. |
| Danish. | Russian. |

N.B. — Single poems have been translated into other languages.

**Selections from Longfellow's Early Poems.**

*(Before 1839.)*

An April Day.
Woods in Winter.
Sunrise on the Hills.
Spirit of Poetry.
Hymn of the Moravian Nuns.

**Selections from Longfellow's Later Poems.**

*(After 1839.)*

DRAMATIC POEMS.

The Golden Legend.
The Divine Tragedy.

LONG NARRATIVE POEMS.

Evangeline.
The Hanging of the Crane.
Kéramos.

**Poems of New England Life.**

Courtship of Miles Standish.
The Phantom Ship.
Paul Revere's Ride.
Lady Wentworth.
Elizabeth.
The Rhyme of Sir Cnristopher.

### Poems Inspired by Foreign Life.

Belfry at Bruges.                    Nuremberg.
Amalfi.

### Poems of Life and Death.

The Reaper and the Flowers.
Midnight Mass of the Dying Year.
The Goblet of Life.
Endymion.
Resignation.
The Builders.
The Ladder of Saint Augustine.
Haunted Houses.

### Poems on Human Slavery.

The Slave's Dream.
The Slave singing at Midnight.
The Warning.

### Sea Poems.

The Building of the Ship.
Sir Humphrey Gilbert.
The Fire of Drift-wood.
The Bells of Lynn.
The Tide rises, the Tide falls.

### Nature Poems.

Autumn.
Hymn to the Night.
Flowers.
Rain in Summer.
Snow Flakes.
The Birds of Killingworth.
Flower de Luce.

## Personal Poems.

The Fiftieth Birthday of Agassiz.
Hawthorne.
Charles Sumner.
The Herons of Elmwood.
In a Churchyard at Tarrytown.   (To Irving.)
The Three Silences of Molinos.   (To J. G. Whittier.)
Walpentake.   (To Alfred Tennyson.)
Bayard Taylor.

## Ballads.

The Skeleton in Armor.
The Wreck of the Hesperus.

## Indian Tradition.

Burial of the Minnesink.
To the Driving Cloud.
The Song of Hiawatha.

## Selections from Hiawatha.

"Young and beautiful was Wahan,"      Canto II.
" Forth into the forest straightway,"          "      III.
"Two good friends had Hiawatha,"          "      VI.
" Give me of your bark, O birch tree,"      "      VII.
" As unto the bow the cord is,"                "      X.
The death of Kwasind,                          "      XVIII.
The famine,                                          "      XX.
Hiawatha's departure,                          "      XXII.

The Revenge of Rain-in-the-Face.

## Sonnets.

Dante.                          Chaucer.
Keats.                          The Old Bridge at Florence.
Giotto's Tower.          President Garfield.

**Miscellaneous Lyrics.**

Excelsior.
The Village Blacksmith.
The Bridge.
The Day is Done.
The Arrow and the Song.

**Translations.**

Dante's Divina Commedia.   1867–1870.
Children of the Lord's Supper.   1841.
Tomorrow.
The Grave.
Song of the Silent Land.

**A Group of Translators of Dante.**

Rev. Henry Boyd.   1802.
Henry Francis Cary.   1806–1814.
John Dayman.   1843–1864.
Henry Wadsworth Longfellow.   1867–1870.
William Michael Rossetti.   1869.
Ichabod Charles Wright.   1872.
E. H. Plumptre.   1887.

NOTE. — For other translators see Willard Fisk's Bibliography of
Dante.

**Selections from Prose Writings.**

Defence of Poetry.   North American Review.   1832.
Outre Mer.   1835.
Hyperion.   1839.
Poets and Poetry of Europe.   1845.
Kavanagh.   1849.

**Selected Books of Reference on Longfellow and his Works.**

Outre Mer. By O. W. B. Peabody. North American
Review. October, 1834.

Hyperion. By C. C. Felton. North American Review.
January, 1840.

Longfellow's Ballads and Other Poems. By C. C. Felton.
North American Review. July, 1842.

A Fable for the Critics. By James Russell Lowell. 1848.

Evangeline. By C. C. Felton. North American Review.
January, 1848.

Nationality in Literature. (Kavanagh.) By James Russell
Lowell. North American Review. July, 1849.

Literati. (Mr. Longfellow and Other Plagiarists.) By E. A.
Poe. (For an answer to this, see Underwood's Longfellow. Chapter on Criticism.)

Longfellow's Golden Legend. (A criticism on the resem-
blance of the Golden Legend to Faust.) Blackwood's
Magazine. February, 1852.

Comparison of Faust and the Golden Legend. Fraser's
Magazine. April, 1853.

Longfellow's Works. By a Catholic Reviewer. Dublin
Review. June, 1853.

The Song of Hiawatha : a Review. By E. E. Hale. North
American Review. January, 1856.

Longfellow. By George W. Curtis. Atlantic Monthly.
December, 1863.

Tales of a Wayside Inn. British Quarterly Review.
January, 1864.

Henry Wadsworth Longfellow. By W. D. Howells. North
American Review. April, 1867.

Mr. Longfellow's Translation of the Divine Comedy. The
Nation. May 9 and June 20, 1867. (The second article gives
comparison with other translations of the same passages.)

The Divine Comedy : a Review. By Charles Eliot Norton. North American Review. July, 1867.

Literary Recreations and Miscellanies. (Evangeline.) By J. G. Whittier. 1872.

English Poets. (Longfellow.) By J. Gostwick. 1875.

Longfellow and his Works. By Ray Palmer. International Review. November, 1875.

Afternoons with the Poets. By C. H. Deshler. 1879.

Henry Wadsworth Longfellow. By Anthony Trollope. North American Review. April, 1881.

Henry Wadsworth Longfellow and his Work. By Lyman Abbott. Supplement to Christian Union. February 23, 1881.

Longfellow. The Literary World. February 26, 1881.

Longfellow. The Springfield Republican. March 25, 1882.

Longfellow. By G. W. Curtis. Harper's Magazine. June, 1882.

The Puritan Element in Longfellow. British Quarterly Review. July and October, 1882.

A Study of Longfellow. Fortnightly Review. January, 1883.

Poets of America. By E. C. Stedman. 1885.

Three Americans and Three Englishmen. (Longfellow.) By C. F. Johnson. 1886.

An English Review of the Life of Longfellow. By Samuel Longfellow. Macmillan's Magazine. May, 1886.

An American Review of the Life of Longfellow. By Samuel Longfellow. Atlantic Monthly. May, 1886.

Men and Letters. (The Art of Longfellow.) By H. E. Scudder. 1887.

# A Guide to the Study of Nineteenth Century Authors.

By LOUISE MANNING HODGKINS,

PROFESSOR OF ENGLISH LITERATURE IN WELLESLEY COLLEGE.

---

## JOHN GREENLEAF WHITTIER, 1807-.

NOTE. — Whittier is called

The Quaker Poet.
The Wood-thrush of Amesbury.
The Poet of New England History.
The Prophet Bard of America.
The Boanerges of American Poets.
The Hebrew Poet of the Nineteenth Century.
The Poet of the Great Anti-Slavery Reform.
The National Poet of America.

### Significant Facts in the Life of Whittier.

By birth and choice a Friend.
Desultory education.   (Two years at Haverhill Academy.)
First poet read and loved by Whittier, Burns.
First poem published by Whittier, Sicilian Vespers.   (Now out of print.)   First Volume of Poems.   1831.
Mobbed for his anti-slavery opinions in Concord, N.H.  1835.
Massachusetts State Representative.   1835–1836.
Secretary of American Anti-Slavery Association.   1836.

Editorial connection with anti-slavery newspapers. (Most important, Washington National Era. 1847.)
Retired life in Amesbury and Danvers, Mass. 1840-.
First complete edition of Whittier's Poems. 1857.
Member of the Board of Overseers of Harvard College.

NOTE. — It is to be remarked that Whittier has had no collegiate training, has not travelled out of his own country, and has never married.

### Biographical Writings.

Fable for Critics. (Whittier.) By J. R. Lowell. 1848.
Poets' Homes. (John G. Whittier.) By R. H. Stoddard. 1879.
John Greenleaf Whittier. His Life, Genius, and Writings. By W. S. Kennedy. 1882.
The Local Associations of Whittier's Poems. By George M. White. Harper's Magazine. February, 1883.
John Greenleaf Whittier. A Biography. By F. H. Underwood. 1883.
Pall Mall Gazette. November, 1884.
Autobiographic Sketch. Boston Daily Advertiser. December 17, 1887.

### Selected Poems on Whittier.

The Three Silences of Molinos. By H. W. Longfellow.
On Whittier's Birthday. For both the Seventieth and Eightieth Birthdays. By Oliver Wendell Holmes.
Ad Vigilem. By Edmund Clarence Stedman.
John Greenleaf Whittier. A Sonnet. By Paul Hamilton Hayne.
"Poet and Friend, beloved of us so long." By Louise Chandler Moulton.
See also the Literary World for December 17, 1877. The Boston Daily Advertiser for December 17, 1887.

### Poems of Indian Tradition.

Bridal of Pennacook.                    Mogg Megone.

### Poems of Colonial Life.

Mary Garvin.                            Parson Avery.
John Underhill.                         Amy Wentworth.
The Prophecy of Samuel Sewall.          The Preacher.
Skipper Ireson's Ride.                  Abraham Davenport.

### Poems illustrating Whittier's Love of Freedom.

#### ON THE PERSECUTIONS OF THE QUAKERS.

Cassandra Southwick.
The Exiles.
The Old South.
The King's Missive.
How the Women went from Dover.
Banished from Massachusetts.

#### ON FREEDOM AND SLAVERY.

Toussaint l'Ouverture.
Oh, Thou whose Presence went before !
The Farewell of a Virginia Slave Mother.
The Moral Warfare.
Massachusetts to Virginia.
The Reformer.
Men of the Northland.
Randolph of Roanoke.
The Legend of St. Mark's.
John Brown of Ossawatomie.
The Eve of Election.
The Proclamation.
Barbara Frietchie.
Laus Deo !

## A Group of Famous Anti-Slavery Men and Women.

Samuel Hopkins.
William Leggett.
Elizur Wright.
William Ellery Channing, Sr.
Nathaniel Peabody Rogers.
John G. Whittier.
Lydia Maria Child.
Angelina Grimke Weld.

The Beechers.
Charles Sumner.
Henry Wilson.
Charles B. Storrs.
William Lloyd Garrison.
Wendell Phillips.
Lucy Stone.
Frederick Douglass.

## Personal Poems.

To W. L. G.
Channing.
Ichabod.[1]
Bryant.   On his Birthday.
Thomas Starr King.

The Singer.
Frederika Bremer.
An Artist of the Beautiful.
(To George Fuller.)
Mulford.

## Poems of Life and Death.

The Reward.
Questions of Life.
The Vanishers.
The Common Question.
The Answer.
My Triumph.

My Birthday.
Telling the Bees.
The Shadow and the Light.
Trust.
Revelation.
At Last.

## Poems of Religious Life.

Palestine.
The Crucifixion.
The Vaudois Teacher.

Andrew Rykman's Prayer.
The Cry of a Lost Soul.
The Grave by the Lake.

---

[1] Written when Webster gave his assent to the Fugitive Slave Bill.
March 7, 1850.

My Soul and I.   "Oh, lonely bay of Trinity."
Forgiveness.   "The harp at Nature's ad-
Trinitas.   vent strung."
My Psalm.   The Eternal Goodness.
Thy Will Be Done.   Our Master.
The Waiting.   A Timely Word.

### HEBRAIC POEMS.

Ezekiel.
Wife of Manoah to her Husband.

### Poems of Nature.

A Dream of Summer.   Snow Bound.
The Corn Song.   Among the Hills.
April.   The Tent on the Beach.
Summer by the Lakeside.   Sweet-Fern.
The Barefoot Boy.   Saint Martin's Summer.
The River Path.   Sunset on the Bear Camp.

### Narrative Poems.

Skipper Ireson's Ride.   The Swan Song of Parson Avery
Maud Muller.   The Wreck of Rivermouth.
The Witch's Daughter.   The Changeling.
Norembega.   Saint Gregory's Guest.

### Poems of Occasion.

Reunion at Haverhill Academy.   1885.
Centennial Hymn.
For an Autumn Festival.

### A Collection of Poems Edited by Whittier.

Songs of Three Centuries.

**Selections from Whittier's Prose.**

Margaret Smith's Journal.   (A story of Puritan intolerance.)
John Bunyan.
William Leggett.
The Agency of Evil.
Mirth and Medicine.
Justice and Expediency, or Slavery considered with a View
to Abolition.

**Selected Books of Reference on John Greenleaf Whittier
and his Works.**

Voices of Freedom.   By Daniel March.   New Englander.
January, 1848.
Recollections of a Literary Life.   (American Poets.)   By
Mary Russell Mitford.   1852.
Mental Portraits.   (Whittier.)   By H. T. Tuckerman.   1853.
John Whittier and his Writings.   By J. S. Thayer.   North
American Review.   July, 1854.
Modern Agitators.   (J. G. Whittier.)   By D. W. Bartlett.
1859.
Home Ballads.   Westminster Review.   November–May,
1860–1861.
London Athenæum.   Littell's Living Age.   October 12, 1861.
Whittier.   By D. W. Wasson.   Atlantic Monthly.   March, 1864.
The Tent on the Beach.   By J. R. Dennett.   The Nation.
March 7, 1867.
Three Old and Three New Poets.   (Mabel Martin.)   By
Bayard Taylor.   International Review.   May, 1876.
Afternoons with the Poets.   (Seventh Afternoon.)   By C. D.
Deshler.   1879.
John Greenleaf Whittier.   By R. H. Stoddard.   Scribner's
Monthly.   August, 1879.

American Prose. (For excellent selections from Whittier.) 1880.

Chats about Books, Poets, and Novelists. (Whittier.) By M. W. Hazeltine. 1883.

Whittier and his Verse. By S. N. Thayer. Christian Union. March 6, 1884.

Pall Mall Gazette. 1884.

Poets of America. (Whittier.) By E. C. Stedman. 1886.

American Literature. (Whittier.) By E. P. Whipple. 1887.

Boston Daily Advertiser. (A Whittier Birthday Number.) December 17, 1887.

# A Guide to the Study of Nineteenth Century Authors.

By LOUISE MANNING HODGKINS,

PROFESSOR OF ENGLISH LITERATURE IN WELLESLEY COLLEGE.

Copyright, 1888.

## OLIVER WENDELL HOLMES, 1809-.

NOTE. — Oliver Wendell Holmes is called

The American Montaigne.
The Autocrat of the Breakfast Table.
The Professor of the Breakfast Table.
The Poet of the Breakfast Table.

### Significant Facts in the Life of Oliver Wendell Holmes.

Gentle and Literary Ancestry.

Education at Phillips-Andover Academy and Harvard College. First Degree, 1829.

Abandonment of Legal Profession.

Study and Practice of Medicine. Degree, 1836.

Publication of First Volume of Poems. 1836.

Chair of Anatomy and Physiology in Dartmouth College. 1838–1848.

Chair of Anatomy and Physiology in Harvard College. 1848–1882.

Publication of the Autocrat at the Breakfast Table. 1858.

The Holmes Birthday Breakfast. 1879.

Celebration of the Seventy-fifth Birthday. 1884.

Second Visit to Europe, after an interval of fifty years. 1886.
D.C.L. of Oxford, England, and LL.D. of Edinburgh. 1886.
Retired Life in Boston, Mass.

NOTE. — "Dr. Holmes bears much the same relation to Boston that
Dr. Johnson did to London." — C. F. JOHNSON.

### A Group of Dr. Holmes's Classmates at Harvard.

| | |
|---|---|
| Judge B. R. Curtis. | James Freeman Clarke. |
| George T. Bigelow. | Chandler Robbins. |
| George T. Davis. | William Henry Channing. |
| Professor Benjamin Pierce. | Rev. S. F. Smith. |

NOTE. — Poems of occasion written for the Class of '29 contain
many allusions to the names in this list.

### Biographical Writings.

Oliver Wendell Holmes. By Francis H. Underwood.
Scribner's Monthly. May, 1879.
American Prose. (Oliver Wendell Holmes.) 1880.
Oliver Wendell Holmes. By William Sloane Kennedy. 1883.
Life of Dr. Holmes. By E. E. Brown. 1884.
Famous American Authors. By Sarah K. Bolton. 1887.

### Writings contributing to his own Biography.

Parson Turell's Legacy.
The Opening of the Piano.
First Chapter of Poet at the Breakfast Table.
Dorothy Q.
A Family Record.
The Iron Gate. (Poem of his Seventieth Birthday.)
The School Boy.
Introduction to A Moral Antipathy.
Personal Allusions in Poems of the Class of '29.

## PROSE WORKS OF DR. HOLMES.

NOTE.— Dr. Holmes is noted as a scholar, scientist, satirist, humorist, wit, essayist, novelist, biographer, lecturer, poet.

### Criticisms.

Autocrat of the Breakfast Table.   1858.
Professor at the Breakfast Table.   1859.
Poet at the Breakfast Table.   1873.

### Romances.

Elsie Venner.   1860.
Guardian Angel.   1867.
A Moral Antipathy.   1886.

### Scientific Writings.

Currents and Counter-Currents in Medical Science.   1861.
Border-Lines in Medical Science.   1862.
Mechanism in Thought and Morals.   1871.

### Memoirs.

Memoir of John Lothrop Motley.   1879.
Memoir of Emerson.   (American Men of Letters Series.)
1884.

### Essay.

Pillow-smoothing Authors.   Atlantic Monthly.   1883.

### Travels.

One Hundred Days in Europe.   1887.

### Miscellaneous Writings.

Soundings from the Atlantic.   1864.

NOTE. — Much of Dr. Holmes's work was originally contributed to
the Atlantic Monthly, which he named.

SELECTIONS FROM DR. HOLMES'S POEMS.

### Humorous Poems.

The Last Leaf.

My Aunt.

Evening.

The September Gale.

The Height of the Ridiculous.

Contentment.

The One Hoss Shay.

Aunt Tabitha.

Epilogue to the Breakfast Table Series.

A Farewell to Agassiz.

### Patriotic Poems.

Old Ironsides.

Lexington.  (In measure of Scott's " Hail to the Chief.")

Our Yankee Girls.

Robinson of Leyden.

A Voice of the Loyal North.

Boston Tea Party.

Grandmother's Story of Bunker Hill.

An Appeal for the Old South.

### Poems of Moral and Spiritual Beauty.

Our Limitations.

A Mother's Secret.

The Voiceless.

The Living Temple.

The Chambered Nautilus.

Under the Violets.

The Crooked Footpath.

Homesick in Heaven.

### Verses for Occasions.

Bill and Joe.  Class of '29.

" Has there any old fellow got mixed with the boys?'

Bryant's Seventieth Birthday.

To H. W. Longfellow.

In Memory of Abraham Lincoln.

Shakespeare Tercentennial Celebration.

Welcome to the Nations.   Philadelphia, July 4, 1876.
The Iron Gate.
For Whittier's Seventieth Birthday.
For the Shakespeare Fountain at Stratford-on-Avon.

### Poems from the Lowell Institute Lectures, 1852.

After a Lecture on Wordsworth.
After a Lecture on Keats.
After a Lecture on Shelley.

### Hymns.

" O Love Divine, that stooped to share."
" Lord of all being, throned afar."
In Memory of Abraham Lincoln.
" Father of Mercies, Heavenly Friend."

### Selected Books of Reference on Oliver Wendell Holmes and his Works.

Holmes's Urania.   By J. G. Palfrey.   North American Review.   January, 1847.

A Fable for the Critics.   By James Russell Lowell.   1848.

Humorous and Satirical Poetry.   North American Review. January, 1849.

Review of Holmes's Poems.   Littell's Living Age.   January 6, 1849.

Mirth and Medicine.   A Review of Holmes's Poems.   By J. G. Whittier.   Littell's Living Age.   March 17, 1849.

American Authorship.   (Oliver Wendell Holmes.)   Littell's Living Age.   October 8, 1853.

American Humour.   North British Review.   August–November, 1860.

Elsie Venner and Silas Marner. By J. M. Ludlow. Macmillan's Magazine. August, 1861.

Dr. Oliver Wendell Holmes and Elsie Venner. The National Review. October, 1861.

The Americans at Home. (Dr. Holmes as a lecturer before his medical classes.) By David Macrae. 1864.

American Prose. (Holmes.) 1880.

Oliver Wendell Holmes. By Ray Palmer. International Review. May, 1880.

The Holmes Breakfast. Atlantic Monthly Supplement. June, 1880.

Pen Pictures of Modern Authors. (Holmes.) The Literary Life. 1882.

American Humourists. (Holmes.) By H. R. Haweis. 1883.

Pall Mall Gazette. November, 1885.

Poets of America. (Oliver Wendell Holmes.) By E. C. Stedman. 1886.

Half-hours with the Best American Authors. By C. Morris. 1886.

American Literature. (O. W. Holmes.) By E. P. Whipple. 1887.

# A Guide to the Study of Nineteenth Century Authors.

### By LOUISE MANNING HODGKINS,

**PROFESSOR OF ENGLISH LITERATURE IN WELLESLEY COLLEGE.**

---

## JAMES RUSSELL LOWELL, 1819–.

### A Pseudonym of Lowell.

Hosea Biglow.

NOTE.— Lowell is called

The Songster of Elmwood.
The Author of the American Hudibras.
Our Ablest Critic.
Our New Theocritus.

### Significant Facts in the Life of James Russell Lowell.

Distinguished Ancestry.
Ancestral Home, Elmwood, Cambridge, Mass.
Education :
Degree of Harvard College.  1838.
Degree of Harvard Law School.  1840.
Publication of First Volume of Poems.  A Year's Life
1841.

5C

Marriage to Maria White. 1844. (Mrs. Lowell died in 1853. Mr. Lowell has been twice married.)
Lecturer before the Lowell Institute. 1854.
Election to Chair of Modern Languages at Harvard College. 1855.
Editor of the Atlantic Monthly. 1857–1861.
Editor, with C. E. Norton, of the North American Review. 1863–1872.
Minister to Spain. 1877–1880.
Minister to England. 1880–1885.
Lecturer before the Lowell Institute. 1886.
Publication of Last Volume of Poems. Heartsease and Rue. 1888.

### Biographical Writings.

Poets' Homes. (Lowell.) By R. H. Stoddard. 1879.
Pen Pictures of Modern Authors. (Lowell.) By William Shepherd. 1882.
James Russell Lowell. A Biographical Sketch. By F. H. Underwood. 1882.
Poets of America. (Lowell.) By Edmund Clarence Stedman. 1885.
Mr. Lowell. The Literary World. June 27, 1885.
Famous American Authors. (Lowell.) By Sarah K. Bolton. 1887.

### Poems of Lowell contributing to his own Biography.

| | |
|---|---|
| Threnodia. | A Fable for Critics. (Lowell.) |
| Irené. | The First Snowfall. |
| The Beggar. | After the Burial. |
| My Love. | The Dead House. |
| A Prayer. | " Past my next mile-stone waits |
| She Came and Went. | my seventieth year." |
| The Changeling. | Sixty-eighth Birthday. |

### Poems on Lowell.

The Herons of Elmwood.  By H. W. Longfellow.
Farewell to James Russell Lowell.  By Oliver Wendell Holmes.
Welcome.  By J. G. Whittier.
To J. R. L.  By C. P. Cranch.
Home-Welcome to Lowell.  By Margaret J. Preston.

NOTE. — For other poems see Literary World, June 27, 1885.

### Sonnets.

"Through suffering and sorrow thou hast passed."
"I ask not for those thoughts that sudden leap."
To the Spirit of Keats.
On Reading Wordsworth's Sonnets.
The Eyes' Treasury.
To Edmund Quincy.

### Poems of Legend and Tradition.

A Legend of Brittany.
An Incident of the Fire at Hamburg.
Ambrose.
The Vision of Sir Launfal.
The Singing Leaves.

### Poems of Nature.

Midnight.
To a Pine Tree.
An Indian Summer Reverie.
The Oak.
The Birch Tree.

To the Dandelion.
Beaver Brook.
Under the Willows
Al Fresco.

## Poems of Humor and Satire.

From a Fable for Critics :

The Portraits of

| | |
|---|---|
| Emerson. | Cooper. |
| Bryant. | Margaret Fuller. |
| Whittier. | Irving. |
| Hawthorne. | |

NOTE — A Fable for Critics is called the American Dunciad.

From the Biglow Papers :

What Mr. Robinson Thinks.
The Debate in the Sennit.
A Second Letter from B. Sawin, Esq.
The Courtin'.
Mason and Slidell : A Yankee Idyll.
Jonathan to John.
Sunthin' in the Pastoral Line.
Mr. Hosea Biglow to the Editor of the Atlantic Monthly.
A Satire upon War and Slavery.

Fitz-Adams' Story.                  Tempora Mutantur.

NOTE — The Biglow Papers was a protest against tyranny, hypocrisy, and disloyalty on the part of the American people. The first series was published in the Boston Courier, 1846.

## A Group of American Wits and Humorists.

Washington Irving.
Sam Slick (Judge Haliburton).  (Nova Scotian.)
O. W. Holmes.

Mrs. Partington (B. P. Shillaber).
John G. Saxe.
Josh Billings (Henry Shaw).
James Russell Lowell.
Charles Dudley Warner.
G. W. Curtis.
Petroleum V. Nasby (D. R. Locke).
Artemus Ward (C. F. Browne).
Mark Twain (Samuel L. Clemens).

**Selections from the Prose Works of Lowell.**

ON NATURE.

My Garden Acquaintance.
A Good Word for Winter.

ON NEW ENGLAND HISTORY.

Witchcraft.
New England Two Centuries Ago.
Cambridge Thirty Years Ago. (1853.)

ON FOREIGN TRAVEL.

In the Mediterranean. Italy.

ON AUTHORS.

Dante. Dryden.
Spenser. Gray.
Shakespeare once more. Emerson as a Lecturer
Milton.

**Selections from Addresses.**

Coleridge. Democracy.
Browning.

### Selected Books of Reference on James Russell Lowell and his Works.

Lowell's Poems. By Margaret Fuller. The Dial, 1841. (An unfavorable criticism.)

Lowell's Poems. A Year's Life. By G. S. Holland. North American Review. April, 1841.

Lowell's Poems. By C. C. Felton. North American Review. April, 1844.

Humorous and Satirical Poetry. (A Fable for Critics.) North American Review. January, 1849.

The Biglow Papers. By D. March. New Englander. February, 1849.

Lowell the Poet. Putnam's Magazine. May, 1853.

American Humour. North British Review. August–November, 1860.

James Russell Lowell and Robert Browning. New Englander. January, 1870.

James Russell Lowell. By John Foster Kirke. Lippincott's Magazine. June, 1871.

Mr. Lowell's Prose. By W. C. Wilkinson. Scribner's Monthly. May, June, July, 1872. (An unfavorable criticism.)

Cambridge on the Charles. By Charles F. Richardson. Harper's Magazine. January, 1876.

American Prose. (Lowell.) 1880.

James Russell Lowell. By Edmund Clarence Stedman. Century Magazine. May, 1882.

American Humourists. (Lowell.) By H. R. Haweis. 1883.

A Welcome to Lowell. The Literary World. June 27, 1885.

Mr. J. R. Lowell. By H. D. Traill. Fortnightly Review. July, 1885.

Outlooks on Society. (Lowell as a Prose Writer.) By E. P. Whipple. 1888.